YOU WERE BORN WITH
PERSONAL POWER
To Be, Do, Or Have ANYTHING You Want
by Homier Moss

AF138941

Getting from A to B;
From where you are to where you want to be.

What if you had the chance to change the direction your life was going, would you take it?

Take a moment and think about the results you are currently getting in life; your health and fitness, your work, your career, your relationships, your financial status. Are you happy with the results you are getting right now?

Remember, if you want to keep getting what you are getting, keep doing what you are doing.

If you are unhappy with the results you are getting right now, you should know that there is another way. Change your way of thinking. The problem is not always the problem. How you think about the problem is the problem. It has been said that insanity is doing the same thing again and again, waiting for new results. Are you doing the same thing again and again with no new results?

Well now it's time to create new strategies to make great things happen in your life. As your A to B Strategy Specialist, I can give you practical steps combined with the real inspiration to get you from where you are to where you want to be.

So tell me ... what is it you REALLY want?

A. Would you like to earn more money?
B. Would you like to dramatically improve your relationships? (or create new, lasting relationships)
C. Would you like to improve your fitness; look better and feel better?
D. Would you like to live a more fulfilling life?
E. Would you like to improve your personal self-image and awareness?

You see, any one of the above is possible for you...and more.

That's right, it's all possible, and trust me - if I can do it, you can do it too! In order to make these things a reality there are three main things you must do:

1. Decide What You Want - Even a vague idea at this time will do, and then you can turn it into a clear and concise goal later.

2. Find A Mentor - Find someone who has achieved a level of success and awareness you're longing for, and model them. Learn from them. You do not need to recreate the wheel, or 'go-it-alone.'

3. Get Moving - If you want something, get moving!! Take the necessary steps every single day to get you closer to your dreams and goals.

As far as mentors, I think a person should ALWAYS have at least one mentor - and, I'd really like to be yours. I know I can show you how to achieve anything you truly desire.

If you want to create success for yourself and achieve your goals and dreams you need to remember this; problem solving is the key. There is always a better way to do things. It's important to know how to get from where you are to where you want to be. Contact me and let me show you how to...

Design Your Life! - How to get from A to B;
from where you are to where you want to be
Fitness | Business | Relationships | Well-being

Homier Moss,
Author, Fitness & Lifestyle Consultant
Contact: homier.mjr@gmail.com

Bibliografische Information der Deutschen Nationalbibliothek:
Die Deutsche Nationalbibliothek verzeichnet diese Publikation
in der Deutschen Nationalbibliografie; detaillierte bibliografische
Daten sind im Internet über http://dnb.dnb.de abrufbar.

Herstellung und Verlag:
BoD - Books on Demand, Norderstedt

ISBN 978-3-7386-5284-0

You Were Born With Personal Power
To Be, Do or Have Anything You Want
by Homier Moss

"Making the simple
complicated
is commonplace;
making the
complicated simple,
awesomely
simple, that's creativity"

Homier Moss
"Your from A to B Strategy Specialist"

Dedicated to You

This book contains dozens of tested
and proven strategies that I have
used for years. You have personal power
and your power is unlimited. You have the
power within you to create the future
life you wish to have.

*We are our own dragons as well as our own heroes,
and we have to rescue ourselves from ourselves.*

Acknowledgments

This has been a long time in the making. I am simply glad I am able to share it with you. The information here has literally helped me make changes in my life and if you make a decision to use it, it will help you make changes in your life. My aim with this book is to put down on paper what I see, what I feel and what I know in the best and simplest way.

A really big Thank you, Thank You, Thank You to my son Malcolm for being there and helping me out the past few years. We have accomplished so much from then until now. And it just keeps getting better. Life is good all the time.

A special thanks to Malvine for being a part of my life and for her ongoing support. Life is good all the time and it's great to be able to share it with someone who cares.

Many great minds of the past and present made it possible for me to write this book; Bob Proctor, Earl Nightingale, Napoleon Hill, Wallace D. Wattles, Buddha, Socrates, Aristotle, James Allen, Rhonda Byrne, Les Brown, Michael Beckwith and many others. Their work made it possible for me to reshaped my life. For that I am very thankful.

TABLE OF CONTENTS

INTRODUCTION

"Your time is limited, so don't waste it living someone's else's life. Don't be trapped by dogma, which is living with the results of other people's thinking. Don't let the noise of other peoples opinion drown out your inner voice. And most important, have the courage to follow your heart and intuition. They somehow know what you truly want to become. Everything else is secondary". Steve Jobs

We all are special. We all have a gift, something that we truly do a great job at, because it's fun when we do it. And it's our duty to take our talents and greatness and share it with the world. That's the reason why we are here.

Now you may have thought you were here to go to school, get a job, get married, pay monthly bills, party on the weekend, then have some kids, and then your kids will have kids, they will call you grandmother or grandfather, you live a little bit, then die.

Well I am sorry but that's just really way too simplistic. There's a lot more to life than that and I am sure you will agree with me on that too. What do you enjoy doing? What do you dream about? Here is even a better question, "Who were you before you started doing things simply because that is what everyone does? Who were you before people started telling you you can't do this and you shouldn't do that - imposing their limited beliefs on you?

I had reached a point were I started to let other people impose their limited beliefs on me. They had me believing that I was wrong all the time and wasn't capable of getting things right.

They lead me to believe that I was a failure. That way of thinking almost ruined my life.

Prior to 2008, my life was good. I was a very successful business man who was always in a good mood. Back then I didn't even know about the law of attraction but I can recall telling myself on a regular basis how great it would be to go out every weekend and get paid for doing so. That thought alone made me very successful in the nightlife entertainment industry. Events, parties, security, bartender, the whole works. I could support my family and pay my bills. I worked hard, I played hard. But most importantly I was happy doing what I doing. People were always amazed with my good mood. People would always ask me, "How do you stay in this good mood all the time?" I could never explain it. For me it was something I did without giving it much thought and 80% of the time I got it right.

It has been said that to be successful you have to be in the right place at the right time. That's true but there is an important part missing. You have to be aware that you are in the right place at the right time. Awareness is everything. And like most people, I was not aware.

In 2008 I was at a point in my life when I was facing challenges from every direction you could think of – family, business; my life began to collapsed around me. My marriage had fallen apart. I was betrayed and deserted by people who I thought loved me and who I thought were family. Everything was in turmoil. The family unit that I enjoyed no longer existed. I was alone, devastated and depressed. I was very successful at what I was doing, but I started letting other peoples opinion of me bring me down. Because of someone else's negative feedback I thought I had failed and was not worthy of the successful life I so wanted to achieve.

Then I read this from James Allen book, As a Man a Thinketh,

We must learn the truth, that WE ARE THE MAKERS OF OURSELVES by virtue of the thoughts we have. The mind is truly the master weaver, bringing together inner character and outer circumstance so that we can take ignorance and pain; and bring it together for enlightenment and happiness.

That was my "aha" moment. The power of thought. If I change my way of thinking then I can change my life. "An interesting concept" I thought to myself.

I realized it was time for a new strategy. I begin reading about how to change my way of thinking.

Today I have a very positive outlook on life. I am very creative and I am constantly reaching new levels of awareness. I am an optimist. I know anything is possible if you really put your heart and mind into it. Once I started to change the way I think my life began to change.

I created my own lifestyle business, increased my income, my relationships improved, I was able to work on my fitness, get in shape and get rid of that extra weight and develop a plan to keep it off. I found my purpose. And day by day it just keeps getting better.

But here is the really cool part. Now I can tell you how I did it!

I am going to be sharing with you things that have worked for me. I am not asking you to believe me, I am not asking you to agree with me. All I am suggesting is that you look at your life, and see if you are happy with the results you are currently getting. If you are, that's fine. Remember: " If you want to keep getting what you're getting, keep doing what you're doing." But if you are not happy with the results you are currently receiving then maybe you will want to look at it from a new perspective and develop a new strategy.

Some of the things that I am going to share with you, you already know. But you are going to have to take it one step farther. To quote Goethe: "Knowing is not enough you have to apply it. Willing is not enough you have to do it. "

The mission is a simple one, I want to represent an idea, show that possibilities do exists, to be magic, to show that you really can make what you want happen. To use my life as an example and prove this with my life. I am going to set a goal, get a dream, have a vision of myself that will take me out of my comfort zone. I will THINK BIG and set a goal so high that someone would say "That's impossible, you can't do that!" but it will be something that I love and enjoy doing. If I can go out there and make my dream happen, then you can go out there and make your dream happen.

How to use this book

This book is designed to give you simple instructions on how to change your life. I would suggest you read this book from start to finish first. Make your notes and re-read sections of interest on a re-occurring basis. You should learn and master each task presented here if you want to reinvent your life. But the order in which you learn them is not important. Pick out a subject that is of interest to you and start there. Each week learn and master a new technique. I would recommend that you place extra focus on chapters: The Magic Word, Choice and Decision.

Something else you need to keep in mind. You will need to read this book more than one time. You will actually need to read it five times. Most people will read it once and say "I understand it", which they will, but they will never apply it.

When you read a good book a second time you do not see something in the book that was not there before. You see something in yourself that was not there before.

Besides, everything you have learned up to now has been based on the "repeat process". You know your name only because as a child you were constantly called that name and after time you accepted it as yours.

What's your favorite song?

Yes, that's right, what is your favorite song? You know, the one you like to hear and sing to almost everyday. Think about it for a moment. I am talking about the song that you know ALL the words to. Do you have it now? Ok good, now how did you learn the words to that song?

Well chances are you have your favorite song on your smartphone, MP3 player or CD. And every chance you get you play it. When you are by yourself, like alone in your car or you have you headphones on while riding public transportation you play it five or six times in a row. Probably even more. It is through the repeat process of hearing your favorite song over and over again that you now know it from beginning to end with no problem.

Learning new techniques to change your life are learned in the same way, through the art of repetition.

Now let's get started.

Key To Success

Here is the big question that I have spent years on trying to find an answer to: Is there a key to success? I mean a key to success that EVERYBODY can use. A key to success that the only requirement is that you simply be made aware of it and then use it. Is there such a key?

YES, there is such a key and I am going to share it with you.

Here is the key to success...and by the way, this is also the key to failure.

That secret, magic key to success is THE POWER OF THOUGHT.

We become what we think about.

The power of thought has actually been around for over two thousand years. Buddha even speaks on the power of thought:

"We are what we think. All that we are arises with our thoughts. With our thoughts, we make the world."

And...

„ To enjoy good health, to bring true happiness to one's family, to bring peace to all, one must first discipline and control one's own mind. If a man can control his mind he can find the way to Enlightenment, and all wisdom and virtue will naturally come to him."

As you read the material in this book you will be asked to do things you do not normally do. Keep in mind you're developing

19

a new strategy because the one you are currently using does not work. This takes time and practice. Practice does not make you perfect. Practice makes you a better person by allowing you to improve on yourself day by day.

Impossible means I'm possible

Whatever obstacle you face, you will get through it. Remember:

Whether you think you can,
or whether you think you can not,
You're right!

That's your key to success.

What's Necessary

When people have problems it usually has something to do with one or more of the following issues:

1. Weight. Being over weight and/or out of shape. A health related issue.
2. Relationships. The important people in your life.
3. Work. Spending time doing something they really do not enjoy.
4. Money. How to get more of it.

A problem in just one of these areas makes your life very uncomfortable. Having a problem in one or more areas makes your life seem hard. It's not enjoyable and the stress of it all gives you the feeling of moving around in circles, with no solution in site.

Most people do make an effort to try and change things. They will try something and it doesn't work. They wait a while and try again. It doesn't work. They take what they know and work with it as best as they can. A person will try to do something only 2 or 3 times and when it doesn't work they say: "That's the way it was, that's the way it is, and that's the way it always will be".

Albert Einstein stated that insanity is "doing the same thing over and over and the waiting for new results."

Unfortunately that's what people do. The problem is not the problem. How you think about the problem, that's the problem. The solution would be to find a new strategy for getting things done. Here is what's necessary for you to know to get started.

1. Whatever you want to be, do or have, the first person who has to believe it is you. You don't need a plan B because it will distract you from plan A.

2. Know that it is possible. You may not know how but you do know it's possible.

3. You and I, and every successful person on this planet have one thing in common; we all have 24 hours a day. Successful people are not people without problems. Successful people are people who have learned to solve their problems.

4. There is no such thing as "time management." You do not management time, you manage your priorities. You do that with time boxing or advanced decision making.

5. You are going to have to discipline yourself more. Discipline is a command that you give to yourself and you have to follow it.

6. You are going to have to sacrifice. Sacrifice is not just about giving up something. Sacrifice is about giving up something on a lower level to obtain something on a higher level.

7. There is a Law of Attraction, what you think about you bring about. More on this later.

8. Re-read good material like this book at least 5 times and integrate it in your life.

9. Write things down. Start a journal for your dreams, your thoughts, your goals and the steps you are taking to reach them.

10. 100% responsibility - You are responsible for your life. No one else, just you.

Everything is this book is designed so that everyone can use it. There is abundance out there for everyone. Even though everyone can use these techniques most people won't. But I know YOU will.

Are you happy with the results your are currently getting?

Remember, to change your life you have to change your life.

The Magic Word

I have come to learn that words and how we use them play a very important role in our day to day actions. The most important word, in this or any other language, that has a lot to do with the results we receive in life, is the word ATTITUDE.

The dictionary defines Attitude as: "a position of the body or manner of carrying oneself, a state of mind or a feeling." So our moods, feelings and actions have a great effect on how other people relate to us. Our attitude is also an important factor in our success or failure.

Our attitude towards life will determine life's attitude toward us. What I mean is this; Good attitude = good results. Fair attitude = fair results. Bad attitude = bad results. It's really that simple.

You see, if a person has a bad attitude, well they are not going to accomplish much in life. If someone has a poor attitude about school and learning, they will not learn anything until they change their attitude. If you are starting a project and have an attitude of failure within you, you are beaten before you even get started!

William James, who spent almost his entire academic career at Harvard, stated that the greatest discovery of his generation was that „HUMAN BEINGS CAN ALTER THEIR LIVES BY ALTERING THIER ATTITUDES OF MIND." That is another way of saying:

> „By changing your way of thinking,
> you can change your life."

Now if this is so simple, why don't more people do it? And the answer is, they don't know how and they don't believe that it's possible. So William James was right, a change in attitude can change your life.

So how do you go about doing that? Well to develop a good attitude toward other people and the world, you must first develop a good attitude about yourself. It's really hard to give someone something, when you don't have it yourself. If you have a good attitude about yourself, that will effect your attitude towards other people and the world around you.

I have seen this often enough and I know you have too; someone who doesn't like themselves, who is always unhappy about something, will also have a very bad attitude toward other people. A person who is always unhappy and frustrated all the time, is a magnet for unpleasant experiences. On the other hand, a person with a good attitude about themselves, has more happy and pleasant experiences in life. So we need to spend more time making sure we have a good attitude, but we don't. Why?

Well one reason is that we have become so accustomed and familiar with ourselves that we take ourselves for granted. That is, we believe and tell ourselves that there are things that we can not accomplish. But for some really strange reason, we believe others can achieve things that we can not. We simply forget that there is a large amount undeveloped potential in everyone of us – a great sea of talent and ability that we fail to use.

There are people living unhappy, frustrated lives – living defensively, because they have adapted a bad attitude about themselves and towards life. That attitude is the reflection of a person. What's going on the inside will show up on the outside. Every time.

Now let's take a look at successful people, people who go from one success directly to another one. People who may fail at something but shake it off, pick themselves up and move right along to even more success. It's all about ATTITUDE.

It doesn't matter what a person does; people in sales, business executives, doctors, lawyers, housewife or mother. Students, military personnel, people who work in public offices, restaurants and cafes. Literally people in all types jobs in various categories; wherever you find a person doing an outstanding job with fantastic results, you will find a person with the right kind of attitude. These people take on the attitude that they can be, do, or have anything they want. They have the attitude that they can achieve their goals; that it is the natural order of things to be successful. They have a happy, healthy and affirmative attitude about themselves, about life and about the goals they want to accomplish. And because that is how they think, they go out and do wonderful, remarkable and successful things. Other people begin to call them successful, intelligent, brilliant, talented and lucky.

The truth is these people have the same abilities and talent as you and I, and the majority of other people on the planet. What's the difference? They have the RIGHT ATTITUDE. They know it's possible. If you want to do something great and successful, you have to take on the attitude that there are more reasons why you can do it then why you can't. If you want something bad enough, work hard for it, go after it, ask for it, you never give up trying to get it and in most cases it will end up being yours.

This is worth repeating: To change your life, you must change your life. Your attitude creates your environment. Your environment is a mirror of your attitude. You don't like you environment? Change your attitude.

Ok, so if the right type of attitude brings you success, how do you go about getting this type of attitude? One easy and effective way is by „acting as if." If you want to have a good and positive attitude towards life, start acting and carrying yourself as if you have it.

One of the best quotes I have read on this issue comes from Andrew Carnegie:

„Any idea that is held in the mind, that is either feared or revered will begin at one to clothe itself in the most convenient and appropriate form available."

So, if you believe life is dull then you will have a dull, uninteresting life and will become a dull person. If on the other hand you believe that life is interesting, successful and that anything is possible, you will have a great successful life and go on to do many great and wonderful things. It's all about attitude. First, you must mentally become the person you wish to be.

„Before you can do something, you must first be something."
(Goethe)

I am sure you know people who are very often called „lucky." They make life seem simple and go on to do beautiful things with their life and get more things done in one year than most people do in five years.

Right here I am going to share with you a technique that I recommend you use daily. If you focus and work on this technique everyday you will soon find yourself doing interesting, beautiful and successful things. In fact you may just find yourself becoming „lucky."

Most commonly referred to as „The Golden Rule", You should treat others the way you want to be treated. If you want more success in what you are doing, act as if you already have this success in your possession. If you want others to treat you with respect, treat others with respect...FIRST.

TREAT EVERY PERSON AS IF THEY ARE THE MOST IMPORTANT PERSON ON THE PLANET.

And here are three reasons why you should do this:

1. As for as that person is concerned, they think of themselves as being the most important person on the planet.

2. Treating each other as being important and with respect is the way we ought to be treating each other.

3. Once you begin treating everyone this way, you form an important habit.

You see, there is one thing that every man, woman and child wants and needs more than anything else and that is self esteem. That feeling that they are important, that they are needed and respected. They will give their love, respect and support to the person that can fill this need.

28

If you want the world to give you respect and success, give the people of the world that respect and that feeling of success that you would like to have. Wake up each and every morning with the attitude of doing good. Have a smile on your face. If you do it often enough it becomes a habit. You will be more at ease and comfortable with yourself. Irritations that use to frustrate and annoy you will disappear. Whether you are standing in line to buy something or driving your car and someone cuts in front of you or use some other manner that shows their ignorance and lack of courtesy – do not drop to their level. You will not let their unhappiness make you unhappy. By developing a better attitude, it makes you a better person and puts you on your way to achieving those things you want out of life.

As you start your day and through out the day – everyday, here are some things you need to remember:

1. Your attitude at start of what you want to do, will be responsible for its successful outcome.

2. Your attitude to other people will determine their attitude to you.

3. You are what you think. You must „act as if." That is you must think, act, talk, handle and carry yourself as would the person you would like to be.

4. Self esteem; everyone wants to be needed and feel wanted. Treat everyone you meet as an important person, both of you will benefit from it.

5. You can only hold on to one thought at a time so make sure

you keep good thoughts and think positive and affirmative. Always be on alert for new ideas that you can use to make your life better.

Also, very, very important, do not spend your time talking about your problems or about how bad your health is. Unless of course you are talking to your doctor. Talking about your problems, all the time, probably won't help you. It cannot help others.

Keep a good attitude. Have confidence in knowing you will succeed. Treat people you come in contact with as important. Do these things everyday and you will do them for the rest of your life.

Choices

Human choice is the greatest power on earth. Uncomfortable and sometimes difficult to accept, we largely choose our lives and circumstances. We choose our jobs or the work we do. We choose our relationships. We choose our friends. We choose the quality of our relationships and friendships. We choose the homes we live in. We choose whether we are rich or poor.

Unquestionably, some events do occur that we didn't choose and had no power over. But these are relatively rare. By and large, the results we now enjoy, or suffer from, are the consequences of our choices. Habitually, we make thousands of little choices every day. Many of these choices are unexamined, for example, what we eat. Do we know why we eat everything that we do? Do we just habitually eat what appears on the plate? Do we consciously choose all the things we say to the partners we are in relationship with?

What makes the difference? Conscious Awareness.

What is awareness? It's the degree of knowledge or understanding that we have to recognize, both consciously and unconsciously, on all the things that affect our lives.

I used to sit, wonder and ask myself, "Why aren't people trying to better themselves and achieve more out of life? The answer that I found was, most people are simply not consciously aware of the many things that affect their lives and how much control they have over these things. They believe that it was like that in the past, it is like that now and will always be like that in the future. And they just stay in their familiar "comfort zone" and never change.

I have reached a point were I believe that it's ok for people to stay in their comfort zone, if that's what they want to do. These are people who are happy where they are or don't know or believe that they have control over their conscious choices.

So the next question could logically be, "Why were we not built with total conscious to start with?" That's because we have total freedom. Freedom to discover things on our own. If we did not have that, we would not be free. We are free to fall down and be hurt, we then learn from that. If you are bored enough, you are free to learn new things, to even take on risks and then through faith succeed.

Becoming aware means making choices. BETTER choices. The choices you make, whether consciously or unconsciously, will affect your life. YOU are responsible for the choices you make. Your job, the clothes you wear, your relationships, the amount of money you have in the bank, if you are smarter now than you were last year, these are all results from choices that YOU have made. You are either happy or sad because you choose to be so.

We literally have thousands of choices everyday and most people don't even realize this. Most people get in their "comfort zones" and get stuck there. The main reason for staying stuck in a comfort zone is fear. To break out of a comfort zone means doing something new and that scares a lot of people. I am quite sure you have heard of people who stay in bad, abusive marriages because they are afraid to change their situation even though they know they are not happy where they currently are.

Trust me, I know and understand this. I was in a comfort zone too. But once I reached a new state of awareness and became aware of this, it was time to set higher goals and do bigger and better things.

Very many people are unconscious of the fact that are stuck in old beliefs, old customs and old habits. How much of what you do now is based on an old routine that you have been carrying out for years.

I am a big fan of traditions, I think they are great. As long as we do not forget the meaning behind them. I love the Christmas traditions I grew up with but I never forget why we celebrate it. But some people have a routine habit of worrying and that's not good. People are letting doubt and worry control their lives and they are not even aware of it. Most of the time we're not even aware that we are unaware! We know to some degree that we have choices. But when your awareness level increases, you become conscious of the fact that YOU can choose where you want to go in life.

When I increased my level of awareness, I begin to realize that I am responsible for me. And if things were not going right, then I should sit down and find better ways of doing things. That's personal development. I became aware that I am responsible for the opportunities I didn't take advantage of, my current situation and for my actions.

I am truly thankful that we have choices, that we have the ability to reach new levels of awareness and can use that knowledge to create the life we want; to be, do or have anything we want. When we were kids, the adults in our lives made decisions for us. Now that we are adults, we are responsible for ourselves and make our own decisions. Still there are many people out there who are, consciously or unconsciously, letting other people or circumstances make decisions for them.

Changes in your life begin the moment YOU decide to do something that will make your life better.

Decision

There is a single mental move you can make in a millisecond, and it will solve enormous problems for you. It has the potential to improve almost any personal or business situation you will ever encounter and it could literally move you up the path to incredible success. We have a name for this magic mental activity ... it is called DECISION.

Decisions or the lack of them are responsible for the breaking or making of many a career. Individuals who have become very proficient at making decisions, without being influenced by the opinions of others, are the same people whose annual incomes fall into the six and seven figure category. However, it's not just your income that is affected by decisions; your whole life is dominated by this power. The health of your mind and body, the well-being of your family, your social life, the type of relationships you develop, are all dependent upon your ability to make sound decisions.

You would think anything as important as decision making, when it has such far reaching power would be taught in every school, but it is not. To compound the problem, not only is decision-making missing from the curriculum of our educational institutions, up until recently, it's also been absent from most of the corporate training and human resource programs available.

So, how is a person expected to develop this mental ability? Quite simply, you must do it on your own. However, I think it's important to understand that it's not difficult to learn how to make wise decisions. Armed with the proper information and by subjecting yourself to certain disciplines, you can become a very effective decision maker.

You can virtually eliminate conflict and confusion in your life by becoming proficient at making decisions. Decision making brings order to your mind, and of course, this order is then reflected in your objective world , your results.

James Allen may have been thinking of decisions when he wrote, "We think in secret and it comes to pass. Environment is but our looking glass." No one can see you making decisions but they will almost always see the results of your decisions. The person who fails to develop their ability to make decisions is doomed because indecision sets up internal conflicts which can, without warning, escalate into all out mental and emotional wars. Psychiatrists have a name to describe these internal wars, it is ambivalence. What is ambivalence? A state in which you lack certainty or the ability to make decisions. It is that mental disharmony or disconnect you may feel when having both positive and negative feelings about the same object or person. It's like two people living inside one body and each has opposite feelings toward the same objective.

You do not require a doctorate degree in psychiatry to understand that you are going to have difficulty in your life by permitting your mind to remain in an ambivalent state for any period of time. The person who allows this to exist will become very despondent and virtually incapable of any type of productive activity. It is obvious that anyone who finds themselves in such a mental state is not living; at best, they are merely existing. A decision or a series of decisions would change everything.

A very basic law of the universe is "create or disintegrate". Indecision causes disintegration. How often have you heard a person say, "I don't know what to do." How often have you

36

heard yourself say, "What should I do?" Think about some of the indecisive feelings you and virtually everyone on this planet experience from time to time.

LOVE THEM - LEAVE THEM
QUIT - STAY
DO IT - DON'T DO IT
GO BANKRUPT - NO DON'T
GO TO WORK - WATCH TV
BUY IT - DON'T BUY IT
SAY IT - DON'T SAY IT
TELL THEM - DON'T TELL THEM

Everyone, on occasion, has experienced these feelings of ambivalence. If it happens to you frequently, decide right now to stop it. The cause of ambivalence is indecision, but we must keep in mind that the truth is not always in the appearance of things. Indecision is a cause of ambivalence, however it is a secondary cause, it is not the primary cause. I have been studying the behavior of people who have become very proficient at making decisions for a long time. They all have one thing in common. They have a very strong self image, a high degree of self-esteem. They may be as different as night is to day in numerous other respects, but they certainly possess confidence. Low self-esteem or a lack of confidence is the real culprit here. Decision makers are not afraid of making an error. If and when they make an error in their decision, or fail at something, they have the ability to shrug it off. They learn from the experience but they will never submit to the failure.

Every decision maker was either fortunate enough to have been raised in an environment where decision making was a part of their upbringing, or they developed the ability themselves at a later date. They are aware of something that everyone, who hopes to live a full life, must understand: Decision making is something you cannot avoid.

That is the number one principle of decision making. DECIDE RIGHT WHERE YOU ARE WITH WHATEVER YOU'VE GOT. This is precisely why most people never master this important aspect of life. They permit their resources to dictate if and when a decision will or can be made. When John Kennedy asked Werner Von Braun what it would take to build a rocket that would carry a man to the moon and return him safely to earth, his answer was simple and direct. "The will to do it." President Kennedy never asked if it was possible. He never asked if they could afford it or any one of a thousand other questions, all of which would have at that time been valid questions.

President Kennedy made a decision. He said, we will put a man on the moon and return him safely to earth before the end of the decade. The fact that it had never been done before in all the hundreds of thousands of years of human history was not even a consideration. He DECIDED where he was with what he had. The objective was accomplished in his mind the second he made the decision. It was only a matter of time, which is governed by natural law, before the goal was manifested in form for the whole world to see.

There was a time back in 2009 when things were really rough for me. The separation and divorce proceedings was taking its toll on me. I was depressed, wasn't working on a regularly basis and the bills were piling up because there just was not enough money coming in. My son was living with me and I wanted us both, regardless of the money situation, to be able to enjoy life a little.

One of the first things people do when they have money problems is to cut back. They list all the things they can no longer afford to do, and start living there lives without them. How can you possibly move forward when you are taking so many steps backwards?

My decision at that time was to constantly move forward. At the time my son was enjoying his Capoeira lessons, and I was taking Tango lessons a couple of times a week. It was the only thing that literally made me leave the house. I made a decision not to give that up. I made a decision that I would always have money to make these things happen because it was important. Fact is, if you want something bad enough you will find a (legal) way to make it happen. Birthdays and holidays were worked out the same way. I would ask my son in June what he wanted for his birthday in October and for Christmas. A decision was made in advance to ensure that I was able to make these things happen. My philosophy was if you tell me what you want now, I can make it happen. I did the same with myself. We didn't want much, but it was enough to make life enjoyable and I was able to make that happen. When you have something that you enjoy doing, don't just give it up. Take the time to find a way to make it happen. That decision was how I was able to constantly move forward.

I never let money enter my mind when I am deciding whether I will or will not do something. Whether I can afford it or not is never a consideration. Whether I want to do it or not is the only consideration. You can afford anything, there is an infinite supply of money. All of the money in the world is available to you, when the decision is firmly made. If you need money, you will attract it.

I am well aware there are people who will say that is absurd. You can't just decide to do something if you do not have the necessary resources. And that's fine if that is the way they choose to think. I see that as a very limiting way of thinking. In truth, it probably is not thinking at all. It is very likely an opinion being expressed that was inherited from another older member of their family who did not think either.

Thinking is very important. Decision makers are great thinkers. Do you ever give much consideration to your thoughts? How they affect the various aspects of your life? Although this should be one of our most serious considerations, for many people it is not. There is a very small select few who make any attempt to control or monitor their thoughts.

Anyone who has made a study of the great thinkers, the great decision makers, the achievers of history, will know that they very rarely agreed on anything when it came to the study of human life. However, there was one point on which they were in complete and unanimous agreement and that was, "We become what we think about."

What do you think about? You and I must realize that our thoughts ultimately control every decision we make. You are the sum total of your thoughts. By taking charge this very minute, you can guarantee yourself a good day. You can refuse to let unhappy, negative people or circumstances affect you.

The greatest stumbling block you will encounter when making important decisions in your life is circumstance. We let circumstance get us off the hook when we should be giving it everything we've got. More dreams are shattered and goals lost because of circumstance than any other single factor.

How often have you caught yourself saying, "I would like to do or have this but I can't because..." Whatever follows "because" is the circumstance. Circumstances may cause a detour in your life but you should never permit them to stop you from making important decisions.

Napoleon said, "Circumstances, I make them."

The next time you hear someone say they would like to vacation in Paris, or purchase a particular type of car but they can't because they have no money, explain they don't need the money until they make a decision to go to Paris or purchase the car. When the decision is made, they will figure out a way to get the amount needed. They always do.

Many misguided individuals try something once or twice and if they do not hit the bulls-eye, they feel they are a failure. Failing does not make anyone a failure, but quitting most certainly does. And quitting is a decision. By following that form of reasoning, you would have to say when you make a decision to quit, you make a decision to fail.

There is a great quote from Michael Jordan on failing:

"I've missed more than 9000 shots in my career. I've lost almost 300 games. 26 times, I've been trusted to take the game winning shot and missed. I've failed over and over and over again in my life. And that is why I succeed."

This statement from Napoleon Hill still holds true today; "Before success comes in any person's life, they are sure to meet with much temporary defeat and, perhaps some failures." When defeat overtakes a person, the easiest and the most logical thing to do is to quit. That's exactly what the majority of people do."

Charles F. Kettering said, "When you're inventing, if you flunk 999 times and succeed once, you're in."

That is true of just about any activity you can name. The world will soon forget your failures in light of your achievements. Don't worry about failing, it will toughen you up and get you ready for your big win. Winning is a decision.

At 91, J.C. Penny, founder of the department store named after him, was asked how his eyesight was. He replied that his sight was failing but his vision had never been better. That is really great, isn't it?

When a person has no vision of a better way of life, they automatically put themselves in a prison. They limit themselves to a life without hope. This frequently happens when a person has seriously tried, on a number of occasions, to win, only to meet with failure time after time. Repeated failures can damage a person's self-image and cause them to lose sight of their potential. They therefore make a decision to give up and resign themselves to their fate.

Take the first step in predicting your own prosperous future. Build a mental picture of exactly how you would like to live. Make a firm decision to hold on to that vision and positive ways to improve everything will begin to flow into your mind.

Many people get a beautiful vision of how they would like to live but because they cannot see how they are going to make it all happen, they let the vision go. If they knew how they were going to get it or do it, they would have a plan not a vision. There is no inspiration in a plan but there sure is in a vision. When you get the vision, freeze frame it with a decision and don't worry about how you will do it or where the resources will come from. Charge your decision with enthusiasm, that is important. Refuse to worry about how it will happen.

Advanced Decision Making

We make advanced bookings when we fly somewhere, that is quite common. We make doctor appointments, set up meetings, make dates with friends, all in advance. We make advanced reservations to eliminate any confusion or problems when the time arrives for the journey. We do the same with renting a car, for the same reason. Think of the problems you will eliminate by making many of the decisions you must make well in advance. I'll give you an excellent example.

I am a fitness enthusiast, consultant and personal trainer. I enjoy sharing my knowledge with others. If you are really serious about getting results, I can work with you to help you get there. It's important to have a workout plan and a routine you can regularly follow. However, no fitness program is complete without out a good nutrition plan. You do not have to count calories everyday but you do need to be aware of what you eat and how much you eat everyday.

The best quote ever on nutrition comes from Joseph Pilates, the founder of Pilates. From his book "Return to Life Through Contrology" (1945), Joseph Pilates states:

43

"The principle point to remember with regard to diet is to eat only enough food to restore the "fuel" consumed by the body and to keep enough of it on hand at all times to furnish the extra energy required on occasions beyond our normal needs and to meet unexpected emergencies. Merely eating to satisfy one's lust for good food is both foolish and dangerous to one's health. Such a person cannot ever be truly physically fit."

Here is how I make that work for me on a day to day basis. I am always thinking in advance about what I eat and how much I eat. I know what fills me up based on my daily routine. I eat to give my body energy. I have a few meals that I eat almost everyday. My lunch usually takes place around two o'clock in the afternoon. But I can tell you at seven o'clock in the morning what that's going to be. The decision has been made. When work colleagues bring cake and other desserts to the office because it's their birthday or some other special event, I immediately say "No Thank You" when asked.

I do not have to decide whether I want anything or not. Whether I was hungry or not was not a consideration. A decision had previously been made and my "advanced decision" was well tempered with discipline.

The exact same concept works with a person when they are on a diet to release weight. Their decisions are made in advance. If they are offered a big slice of chocolate cake, they don't have to say, "Gee, that looks good ... I wonder if I should." The decision is made in advance. They say, "No Thank You."

I made a decision a long time ago that I would not participate in discussions of why something cannot be done. The only compensation you will ever receive for participating in or giving energy to that type of discussion is something you do not want. I always find it amazing at the number of seemingly intelligent people who persist in dragging you into these negative brainstorming sessions. In one breath these people tell you they seriously want to accomplish a particular objective. And, in the next breath, they begin talking about why they can't. Think of how much more of life they would enjoy by making a decision that they will no longer participate in that type of negative energy.

The humanistic psychologist, Dr. Abraham Maslow who devoted his life to studying self actualized people, stated very clearly that we should follow our inner guide and not be swayed by the opinion of others or outside circumstances. Maslow's research showed that the decision makers in life had a number of things in common; most importantly, they did work they felt was worthwhile and important. They found work a pleasure, and there was little distinction between work and play. Dr. Maslow said, to be self actualized you must not only be doing work you consider to be important, you must do it well and enjoy it.

Dr. Maslow recorded that these superior performers had values, those qualities in their personalities they considered to be worthwhile and important. Their values were not imposed by society, parents or other people in their lives. They made their own decisions. Like their work, they chose and developed their values themselves.

Your life is important and, at its best, life is short. You have the potential to do anything you choose, and to do it well. But, you must make decisions and when the time for a decision arrives, you must make your decision where you are with what you've got.

45

Let me leave you with the words of two great decision makers, William James and Thomas Edison. William James suggested that, compared to what we ought to be, we are making use of only a small part of our physical and mental resources. Stating this concept broadly, the human individual thus lives far within his limits. He possesses powers of various sorts which he habitually fails to use.

Thomas Edison said, "If we all did the things we are capable of doing, we would literally astound ourselves."

By making a simple decision, the greatest minds of the past are available to you. You can literally learn how to turn your wildest dreams into reality.

Put this valuable information to use and recognize the greatness which exists within you. You have limitless resources of potential and ability waiting to be developed. Start today, there's never any time better than the present. Be all that you are capable of being.

What Is Power?

Let me suggest to you the possibility that power, particularly personal power, the human ability to make things happen, is a topic that is not fully understood. Two-thousand-five-hundred years ago Lao Tzu, a famous Chinese philosopher, said that the biggest problem in the world was that individuals experienced themselves as powerless. Today this is still our biggest problem. Lao Tzu wrote the *Tao Te Ching*, which has been translated many times. One such translation is by R.L. Wing: *The Tao of Power*. Wing said:

"Lao Tzu believed that when people do not have a sense of power they become resentful and uncooperative. Individuals who do not feel personal power feel fear. They fear the unknown because they do not identify with the world outside of themselves; thus their psychic integration is severely damaged and they are a danger to their society. Tyrants do not feel power, they feel frustration and impotency. They wield force, but it is a form of aggression, not authority. On closer inspection, it becomes apparent that individuals who dominate others are, in fact, enslaved by insecurity and are slowly and mysteriously hurt by their own actions. Lao Tzu attributed most of the world's ills to the fact that people do not feel powerful and independent."

Power is a multi-faceted concept. You experience a sense of power when you feel in control of your life. Power is the ability to achieve goals. It is also the ability to influence others. Considerable power comes from the ability to communicate. Power includes enthusiasm and optimism. Your energy level is related to your power. If you can cause things to happen, be the master of your destiny, you have power. Power is related to self-esteem and confidence. The freer you are, the more you tend to experience your power.

47

Above all, and this is so important, personal power is the ability to achieve what you want. More than anything else, it is **personal power that brings you success and happiness.**

Let us make a distinction between "coercive power" and "synergic power." By "coercive power" I mean power that involves violence or the threat of violence. This is the power of the armed robber. It is also the power of government. It is the political power that stems from the barrel of a gun, as Tao said. It is power used over people or against them; power at their expense; power which robs them of power.

The concept "synergic power" is expressed in the book Synergic Power: Beyond Domination and Permissiveness by James H. and Marguerite Craig. Synergic power is power used with people. Power exercised in such a way that it is cumulative. Everyone gains power through the power of everyone else, mutually enhancing power.

That is to say, I have gained power. I have learned how to be the master of my thoughts, stay focused, set goals and go out and achieve them. I have increased my level of awareness; increased my personal power. Now I share that information with you. You increase your level of awareness. You gain power. In essence, that's what this book is all about.

What I see mostly on the faces of people when I am in the city is the look of powerlessness. People believe they have no control over their lives. If a situation is not working right people begin to believe "that's the way it was, that's the way it is and that's the way it will always be." Without a doubt, the biggest barrier to success in almost any endeavor is powerlessness, negativity, helplessness, and inertia. They belong together. The problem is not only our own powerlessness, but also the powerlessness of those around us. There is an old saying that

48

goes "Birds of the same feather flock together." So if you hang around negative people, they will turn you into a negative person and you may not even notice it until it is too late.

Power Statement

By "power statement " I mean what are you doing to improve yourself? What do you want? Do you know what you want and are you asking for it? For example, I would like an apple. I ask my friend, "May I have an apple, please?" My friend gives me an apple. I have achieved the desired result: obtaining an apple. The question "May I have an apple, please?" is a power statement.

The application of power messages begins by figuring out what you want by follow certain steps:
(a) Identify or define a desired result.
(b) Develop or select a power message that may achieve the desired result.
(c) Identify or select person(s) likely to assist you in achieving the desired result.
(d) Do not expect the person(s) to be different or behave differently from the way they are and behave.
(e) Put the power message in the environment of the person(s) you want to influence to bring about the desired result.
(f) Observe what happens. Learn from it what works.
(g) If the desired result has been achieved, that ends the procedure.

Now comes the feedback. If the desired result has not been achieved, any or all of the following steps can be taken:
(a) Ask, "What can I learn from what I did and what happened?"
(b) Choose a different desired result.
(c) Select different or more person(s) to whom to present the

power message.

(d) Repeat the power message or put out many copies of it.

(e) Change and improve the power message.

(f) Develop an entirely different power message.

(g) Ask, "What do I need to improve about myself so I can choose attainable desired results, design effective power messages, and select the appropriate person(s) to whom to present my power messages?)

When our power statements fail to produce desired results, it's not a question of wrong or right. It's all feedback. We need to very consciously and deliberately observe, think, and choose what to do next. If we react automatically, unthinkingly, and emotionally we may make undesirable results turn into even worse results. For example, if you react with anger, the result you produce may get worse and worse; such as a shouting match.

The worst thing you can do when you fail to achieve a desired result, is to blame someone else. When you blame someone else you surrender your power. You are saying your success depends on how others are and how they behave. However when you say, "I will change myself and my power statement" then you operate with power.

Curing Helplessness

Helplessness is the opposite of power. Many people are stuck in helplessness and hopelessness. Helplessness can be a dangerous trap. If you are helpless you also tend to be helpless about your helplessness.

Many (if not most) people have to some extent been conditioned to do nothing. No matter what happens in their life they believe they can do nothing about it. They have accepted this as fact. In Martin E.P. Seligman's book *Helplessness* he refers to this as "learned helplessness."

People have learned that no action they could take would change their outcome. When this happens, people are affected by three important aspects: motivationally, cognitively, and emotionally.

They are not sufficiently motivated to persist in finding a way to make a change. The cognitive link between action and consequence (outcome) had been severed in that persons brain as a result of the conditioning. And the person had become more prone to anxiety.

In the process of learning these lessons and making them a part of my life, I developed an awareness of the causality of my actions. Merriam-Webster dictionary defines "causality" as the idea that something can cause another thing to happen or exist. It's the actions that you take that makes things to happen. The awareness of the causality of my actions is the essence of my personal power. "Awareness of the causality of my actions" is another way of expressing "the cognitive links between my actions and the consequences or results I produce."

Most of us never develop that awareness fully. Most of us grew up with a reduced awareness of the causality of our actions. It's so much easier to blame others, to run to the "authorities" to "save" us or just to do nothing.

In general, the link between action and outcome can be expressed in the form of a simple but very useful formula:

"If I do 'A' under conditions 'B,' then the outcome is 'C', 'D' percent of the time."

Examples: "If I wash my hands with soap and water, after reading the newspaper, the outcome is clean hands 99% of the

51

time." "If I wash my hands with soap and water, after fixing my car, the outcome is clean hands 5% of the time." "If I wash my hands with "super cleaner," soap, and water, after fixing my car, the outcome is clean hands 95% of the time." These hypotheses or predictions are continuously tested and refined. This is the basic way we learn how the world works.

Learning Optimism

The person with a sense of personal power tends to feel optimistic most of the time. When helpless we also tend to feel pessimistic. Just like helplessness is something we learn, we can learn optimism. Helplessness is an "unskill" and optimism is a skill.

Martin E.P. Seligman has also written a superb book *Learned Optimism*. He says: "The optimists and the pessimists: I have been studying them for the past twenty-five years. The defining characteristic of pessimists is that they tend to believe bad events will last a long time, will undermine everything they do, and are their own fault. The optimists, who are confronted with the same hard knocks of this world, think about misfortune in the opposite way. They tend to believe defeat is just a temporary setback, that its causes are confined to this one case. The optimists believe defeat is not their fault: Circumstances, bad luck, or other people brought it about. Such people are unfazed by defeat. Confronted by a bad situation, they perceive it as a challenge and try harder.

These two different ways of thinking do have consequences. Literally hundreds of studies show that pessimists give up more easily and get depressed more often. These experiments also show that optimists do much better in school and college, at work and on the playing field. They regularly exceed the predictions of aptitude tests. When optimists run for office, they are more apt to be elected than pessimists are. Their health is unusually good. They age well, much freer than most of us from the usual physical ills of middle age. Evidence suggests they may even live longer."

Seligman uses the concept "explanatory style" to distinguish between optimist and pessimist. Explanatory style describes how we interpret events or situations and describe them to ourselves. Suppose someone's financial situation is that she owes €50,000. The optimist might say, "I owe €50,000. No big deal." The pessimist might say, "I don't know what I'm going to do. My finances are a mess. I'll never get out of debt."

It is important to make a distinction between the fact and the interpretation or explanation. The fact is: "I owe €50,000." The optimist's interpretation is: "No big deal." The pessimist often doesn't state the fact at all. The pessimist seldom distinguishes between fact and interpretation. In a discussion with the pessimist it might take many minutes before she can simply state the fact: "I owe €50,000, period." The pessimist tends to think that her interpretation or explanation is fact. Her interpretation or explanation tends to render her helpless and pessimistic.

It's all up to you. You can be an optimist or you can be a pessimist. Optimism produces health, healing, energy and power. Pessimism produces just the opposite. But how can we be optimistic when it seems there is no light at the end of the tunnel? You can can do so by remembering and practicing the following:

Optimism is a choice - not an inheritance. Tell yourself: I have the freedom to look at any negative situation and take either a negative or a positive attitude.

I am a human being. That means I can learn. I can establish a plan. I can set goals. And if I set a goal, I will achieve at least part of it - if not all of it.

Change is inevitable. If I'm unemployed right now, I can still be grateful and optimistic - because things will not be the same a year from now. Tough times never last, but tough people do.

I will look at what I have left - not at what I have lost. I will regroup the assets I have to create a smaller, but more solid emotional and financial base. For example, there is a guy, with wife and kids who lost his job. Without his income, they could no longer afford the mortgage payments on their home. They've decided to rent it out and move into less spacious quarters. Lifting an emotional and financial burden.

I will keep my optimism growing by tapping into positive memories. We all have positive memories stored within us that we've forgotten. Recall them - especially your past successes and times you overcame pressing problems. Tap into them. Learn from them. They will bring power into your life.

Calm down. Relax. Think. My advice to thousands of people over the years has been: Never make an irreversible decision at a low point in your life. In the Air Force, pilots in training are taught: "If something terrible happens, what do you do? Nothing! Just think!" Quick decisions are impulsive and reactionary. They will only accelerate the problem.

Practice reacting positively. Believe that every scar can be turned into a star! Positive thoughts produce positive results. Negative thoughts always produce negative results.

Believe that anything is possible! You can improve your future if you set clear goals. Devote more time to achieving those goals. Work harder than you've worked before.

Start small. Think tall. Look over the wall! Don't try to achieve your goals overnight. Take small steps at first but never lose sight of the end result you want. You can shape your future until eventually, the outcome will be terrific.

Make an irreversible, irrevocable and irretrievable commitment to keep a "PMA" toward setbacks, problems, failures, and losses. What's a "PMA?" As multimillionaire W. Clement Stone says, it's a "Positive Mental Attitude!

Your Power, Your Mind

You are what you think. And what you think about the most you will attract to you.

Now take a moment and think about some of the things your mind has brought you. The things you have, your work, your relationships with family and friends and your philosophy of life, all come to you as a result of you using your mind. Your way of thinking makes things happen.

Now think about this, we are not even using all of our mental capacity. We are using much less. Many scientists say we are using a very small fraction of our mental capabilities. We are talking about only 10 percent and less.

So how do we tap into this gigantic potential?

I would suggest that you begin to focus on yourself. Work on developing your personal power and your mind. Learn to be the master of your thoughts.

None of us really has an idea of what our mind is truly capable of doing. Your mind can be compared to a undiscovered gold mine. I can tell you that it does not matter whether you are eighteen or eighty, it is there. If you take the time to work with it, it can work for you. You simply need to use your mind more.

Here is one way of looking at it. Your goal is in the future. Your problem is to close the distance which exists between where you are now and the goal you intend to reach. This is the problem to solve.

Successful people are not people without problems. They are simply people who have learned to solve their problems. Successful living and getting the things we want in life is really an issue of solving the problems that stand between where we are now and the point we want to reach!

No one is without problems, they are a part of our life but we waste a lot time worrying about the wrong problems.

„Often we allow ourselves to be upset by small things we should despise and forget. We lose many irreplaceable hours brooding over grievances that, in a year's time, will be forgotten by us and by everybody. No, let us devote our life to worth while actions and feelings, to great thoughts, real affections and enduring undertakings. (Andre Maurois)

Andre Maurois was right. We spend too much time worrying about the wrong things. Here is a reliable estimate of the things people worry about.

40% - Things that never happen.
30% - Things from the past that can not be changed by all the worry in the world.
12% - Needless worries about our health.
10% - Silly, stupid miscellaneous worries.
 8% - Real, legitimate worries.

So let's add it all together, 92% of the worries that take up valuable time, cause painful mental and emotional stress ARE ABSOLUTELY UNNECESSARY.

And if we take a look at the real, legitimate worries, there are only two kinds: there are problems we can solve and there are problems beyond our ability to personally solve. But lets be honest, most of our problems usually fall into the first group, problems that we can solve, if we will take the time to learn how.

There are millions of people today who feel that they can not get any further in life because of problems. They see problems as road blocks stopping them from getting ahead. It would be much easier to look at a problem as a challenge that needs to be taken care of instead of super wide river or canyon that can never be crossed.

One of the truly great benefits of working with a psychiatrist, psychologist or self help groups is learning that you are not alone. That there are thousands, even millions of other people who have the same problems as you have. So at the end of the day, it is not about problems, which we all have at one time or another, but our ability to solve them.

One of the first things you need to have is a goal. That's so important. Now your problem is how do you achieve it?

You may have a goal to be a graphic designer, be a better sales person, get better grades in school, have a greater income, a beautiful home, take a trip around the world or start your own business. If that is your goal, and you know that „You become what you think about the most" so if you stay with it, YOU WILL REACH YOUR GOAL.

Anything that we will want to achieve in the future will certainly be the result of how we use our mind. And even though all of this is true, the mind is the last place on the planet that the average person will turn to for help.

Take a moment, stop and think about all the things the human mind has accomplished. Many of the tools and services you are using today did not even exist 10 years ago. We are developing quite fast, and it is because of the power of the mind.

To use the power of the mind, you must start with thinking. Which is something that a lot of people are not doing. Earl Nightingale once said „If the average person said what they were thinking, they would be speechless." I smile a lot when I hear that because it is so true. We must never take mental activity for thinking. If you stand back objectively and observe what people are doing or listen what people are saying then it becomes obvious that they are not thinking, because if they were, they would never say what they are saying or do what they are doing. This is often the case when I take public transportation. People just do and say unbelievable things. They are not thinking.

When we think, that is when we come up with new ideas. Every new idea triggers another new idea and that is how we grow. We are now living in an age where advancement is all around us in many different areas and it just keeps getting better.

From landing on the moon to the space shuttle, the highest and widest bridges, how we harness energy, to how we communicate. Everything that you can see and touch, that is not water, grass, or trees, was first created by the power of thought. This is the age of the mind and it is all about thinking. Now let me share a few facts with you and show you how you can get your thinking cap on.

The forty-hour work week has long been the standard, and for many people that has been shorten. That means that the average person has a lot of free time. In fact an enormous amount of free time.

If you were to total up the hours in a year (8,760 hours) and subtract the sleeping hours, based on sleeping 8 hours a night (2,920 hours), that is almost 6,000 hours that a person is awake. With a shorten work week and vacation time, they spend less than 2,000 hours working.

That now leaves a person with 4,000 hours a year (about 10 hours a day) when they are neither working or sleeping. And let's not forget weekends. This is free time which one can do whatever they please – at least the mind is free to think. Now it is time to learn how to take advantage of this to create the amazing results we wish to have in life.

EXERCISING YOUR MIND

I would suggest you take one hour a day, five days a week and devote this hour to training and exercising your mind. Choose one hour a day that you can count on and use regularly. For me it is early in the morning. I get up an extra hour earlier, and get a cup of coffee. Everyone else is still in bed. This is the best time for me to get the mind flowing. Here is a good way to do it.

During this hour, take out a blank sheet of paper. At the top the page write down your goal. Now since our future depends on how well we do what we do, write down as many ideas as you can on how to improve on what you are now doing. The idea here is write down 20 ideas on how you can improve what you are doing. You may not always get 20 ideas but that is ok. One idea is good for starters.

When you are doing this keep these two things in mind:
1. This is not easy
2. Some of your ideas may not be good

I say not easy because this is the beginning stage of starting a new habit. You got to stick with it. You are training your mind to forget about all that crappy, nonsense you have in your thoughts and to start think about ways you can improve your work. Remember write down every idea, no matter how crazy it might seem.

Here is what will happen: some of your ideas will be good and you will want to test them out. But this extra hour is important because you are training your subconscious mind to think about ways to improve your work and your life. Twenty ideas a day, that's 100 ideas a week and you still have the weekends free not to think. Just one hour a day, five days a week totals up to 260 hours a year, and it will still leave you with 3,740 hours a year of free time for fun and relaxation. With this plan you are now thinking about your goal and how to improve on your current performance. Think about this, you now have:

Six 40 hour weeks devoted to THINKING AND PLANNING!

And you will still have 15 hours a day to do as you please!

This is how you rise to the next level. This what successful people do to achieve things. This is what I did to come up with the idea to write this book. When you start each day thinking, your mind will continue to work all day for you. When great ideas pop into your mind, write them down as soon as you can. All you need is ONE GREAT IDEA to improve your work and your life!

Now is the best time to take action. Make a commitment to yourself to be a member of the 06.00 a.m. morning club.

If you wanted to improve your fitness, develop more muscles, you would start a daily exercise program to help you reach your goal. The mind is developed the same way but with much more fantastic results. The mind is powerful and can lift anything. No amount of muscle is more powerful than thought. If one had to depend on their muscles for survival, they probably would have disappeared as did the dinosaurs, and they were without a doubt the most physically powerful creatures that ever lived.

It is the power of thought that has brought us to were we are today. You are now going to be the Captain of your ship. And here are some tips to get you started in the right direction:

1. Start this week spending one hour a day writing down ideas on how to improve on what your are doing. Reaching your goal depends on this. When you start doing this and see the results, you will want to continue the practice.

2. Imagine how much more quality you can bring in your life simply by increasing your mental ability.

3. Successful people are not people without problems, they are simply people who have learned to SOLVE THEIR PROBLEMS.

4. Do not waste valuable time and energy worrying about needless, useless and stupid things. 40% of them will never happen, 30% have already happened and can not be changed, 12% are needless worries about our health, 10% are useless, stupid, miscellaneous worries and only 8% are real. Separate the real from the unnecessary and take the time to solve the

problems WITHIN YOUR ABILITY TO SOLVE.

5. Remember we are where we are today based on the power of thought. It is going to get better when you learn that YOUR MIND has the power to take you where you want to go.

Sometimes we do not realize just how much we are truly capable of doing. Deep within ourselves we have unlimited power and abilities – even genius – that can help us be, do or have anything we want. That is the power of YOUR mind.

Success...What It Is And How To Achieve It

To paraphrase an interview with the Noble Prize winner, Dr. Albert Schweitzer, done many years ago; when the reporter asked „What's wrong with people today?", the great Doctor paused for moment and then replied „People don't think." That's a good point, so let's start there.

Today we live in an age where anything is possible. We as people have looked forward to and dreamed of this era for many thousands of years. This is the age of abundant opportunity, for everyone. The possibilities are truly endless. Anyone can come up with a great idea, stay with it and be a millionaire five times over. Just look at all the things that are possible today that did not even exist ten years ago. Unfortunately, we take this for granted. We live in an era where abundant opportunity exists for everyone but many do not take advantage of this. Do you know why this happens?

Well, lets take a hundred people who all start off even at the age of 25. Do you have any idea what will happen to these people by the time they are 65 years old? These one hundred people who start out even at the age of 25, believe they are going to be successful. If you ask them, they would tell you that they are going to be successful. They have that sparkle in their eyes and that glow about them and believe that life is an adventure and they have big dreams but by the time they reach 65 years only one will be rich. Four will be financially independent. Five will still be working. And the rest will be broke or just managing to get by on the little that they have.

So the question is, why do so many fail? What happened to the sparkle in their eyes? What happened to their dreams, their hopes, their plans? Why is there a large difference in what these people wanted to do and what they actually accomplished?

When we say only 5 percent achieve "success", we have to define what "success" really is. Here is the best definition I could find. Now I live by this statement that I got from Bob Proctor back in 2009. Bob Proctor got it from Earl Nightingale back in the 1960s and Earl Nightingale came across it back in the 1950s...

Success is the progressive realization of a worthy idea.

Take a moment, let it sink in and read it again. Now what does that mean? If a person is doing a job, has a goal and doing something because that's what they set out to do and know in what direction they are going, they are a success. If they are not doing that then they are a failure.

Once again...

Success is the progressive realization of a worthy idea.

Rallo May, a psychiatrist, wrote a book called Man's Search For Himself and in this book he says " the opposite of courage in our society is not cowardice, it is CONFORMITY. And that is the problem we have today, conformity. People doing what everyone else is doing and not knowing why.

Think about it, look around you, look at the large number of people 65 and over, they are broke. This is a large group of people who are dependent on someone for their survival. You know we learn to read by the time we are seven, we learn to make living by the time we are twenty-five and in most cases by that time we are supporting a family and yet by the time we are sixty-five we have not learned how to become financially independent in the most richest, abundant era that exist, why? We CONFORM. We end up acting like the wrong percentage group, the 95% who do not succeed. Why do these people don't succeed? They really do not know. They believe that circumstances, other things and other people, are responsible for their success. They believe that things that happen to them are responsible for their success.

If you ask a group of working people "Why do you work, why do you get up in the morning?", they have no idea. The answer I usually get most of the time is "Everyone goes to work in the morning" and that's the reason they do, because everyone else is doing it. They conform.

So if thats the case then who succeeds? The only person who succeeds is the person who is realizing a worthy idea. It's the person who knows what she wants to be, do or have and then begins to work towards that goal.

I will tell you who the successful people are: The school teacher who is teaching school because that's what she wants to do. Success is the person who wants to a fitness trainer, and is doing a great job being one. The guy who has the vegetable stand, who wants to be able to sell fresh vegetables because that was his decision to do so is a success. When the young lady realizes she has a talent for sales and wants to be the very best sales person in her district because that's what she wants, she's a success. It is also the student who wants finish school with good grades and then goes on to learn graphic design or be a music designer. Success is anyone who is doing a predetermined job because that's what they want, because that's what they decided to do. Unfortunately only a very small select group of people make such decisions. The truth is, we really do not have to compete against each other, we need to be more creative about what we want to do.

For the past 15 years or more, I have seen people succeed and seen people fail. What makes the difference? Is there a key to success? Is there a secret to success that is available to everyone? And if we had access to this "secret key", could we immediately begin to use it to make changes in our lives and achieve the success we would like to have? Well I have found that "secret key" to success.

Have you noticed that when some people fail, they just give up and don't care any more? Yet others go on to achieve great success, time and time again. And isn't strange that many of those who achieve success can not tell you how they do it? That's called unconscious competence. They start out being successful and continue to do so, day after day without knowing why. And as for the person who has failed, have you noticed that they always continue fail?

It's because of goals. Some people have them. Some people don't. People with goals succeed because they know where they are going. Let me give you an example: Think of a ship leaving the harbor, with captain and crew. They have the complete voyage mapped out and planned. The captain and crew know exactly where they are going, how to get there and how long it will take. It has a definite goal. This ship will reach it's destination.

Now, if you take another ship and put it in the harbor, with no captain and crew, no voyage plan, what do you think the chances are of that ship reaching it's destination point? None. Even if it did manage to get out of the harbor, it would eventually crash on shore or against the rocks or in bad weather flip over and sink. Why? It has no destination, no goal, no plan and there is no one there to guide it. This is what happens to people with no goal. They never get to where they want to be because they have no plan.

So why is it people with goals succeed in life and people without goals fail?

Here is the "secret key" to success and it is also key to failure:

We become what we think about.

And...

YOU will become what you think about.

Many great people of wisdom along with great teachers and philosophers through the years have disagreed on many subjects. But on this one subject, they all agree. This is what they have said on subject:

"We are what we think. All that we are is arises with our thoughts. With our thoughts we make the world." Buddha

"A persons life is what his thoughts make of it." Marcus Aurelius, Roman Emperor

"Everything comes if a person will only wait. A human being with a settled purpose must accomplish it, and nothing can resist a will that stake even existence for its fulfillment." Disraeli

"A person is what he thinks about all day long."
Ralf Waldo Emerson

"The greatest discovery of my generation is that human beings can alter their lives by altering their attitudes of mind."
William James

"This is one of the greatest laws of the universe. It's as simple as this: If you think in negative terms, you will get negative results. If you think in positive terms, you will achieve positive results. That is a simple fact."
Norman Vincent Peale

"People are aways blaming their circumstances for what they are. I don't believe in circumstances. The people who get on in this world are the people who get up and look for the circumstances they want, and if they don't find them, they make them."
George Bernard Shaw

Well that's what it comes down to. We become what we think about. A person who has a goal that means something to them is going to reach it, because that's all they think about. The person who has no goal, who doesn't know where he's going and whose thoughts are of confusion, anxiety, fear, and worry will create for themselves a life of confusion, anxiety, fear, and worry. If that person thinks about nothing, they become nothing.

Let me explain it another way...

Your mind is similar to the land that a farmer owns. The land gives the farmer the option of choosing what he wants to plant.

The land doesn't care what is planted. The farmer can plant on his land whatever he wants. The farmer just has to make a decision of what to plant.

Your mind, like the land will return what YOU plant in it, but it doesn't care what you plant.

Now the farmer has two types of seeds - one is corn, the other is Belladonna / Nightshade, a very poisonous plant. The farmer plants the seeds, waters and takes care of the land. What do you think will happen?

Like I said, the land does not care. The land will return beautiful rows of Belladonna/Nightshade or beautiful rows of corn. What to plant, or not to plant was the decision of the farmer.

Your mind is a lot more fertile, powerful and incredible than the land but it works the same way. Your mind doesn't care what you plant in it; success or failure. A passionate, meaningful goal or fear, misunderstanding, confusion and anxiety. But whatever you plant it will return back to you.

Our mind is the last great unexplored continent on earth, it contains possibilities and riches far beyond our wildest dreams. And it will return anything we plant in it.

You may wondering, "If all this is true, then why don't people use their mind more.?" Our mind comes to us at birth, it's our standard equipment. It's free. Things that are given to us for free we place little value on it. Oddly enough however, the things we pay for we value. Most people believe that their car is their most valuable asset and not realize that with their mind they can create an idea that is capable earning them thousands

70

or millions of Euros.

It is the things we have gotten for free; our minds, our bodies, our souls, our intelligence, our dreams, the love we have for the people around us, these things are priceless and free. Most people forget to "think about" and "thank about" this.

Anything that costs us money is cheap and can be replaced at any time. A good person can lose their fortune and turn around and make another one. They can do this several times. Many people have done this. If a house burns down, we can rebuild it. Your home, your money, your car; it can all be replaced. It's the things we have gotten for free that we can never replace.

Our mind can do ANY type of job we assign to it. but we end up using it for small unimportant things instead of using it to develop great powerful ideas.

You have to know what you want. Do you want to be promoted within your company? Do you want to have a lot more money than you have right now? Well if you focus on that goal, plant that seed in your mind and care for it, take action steps towards it, you will achieve it. It will become a reality.

Always think about your goal but do it in a relaxed and positive way. Visualize yourself as having already achieved this goal. See yourself doing the things you want to do when you achieve this goal. For every one of us, we become that which we think most often about. We are where we are right now because this is where we really want to be or feel we deserve to be. Most people may choose not to believe that but it is true.

Creating your future is based on the thoughts you have today.

71

What you think today, tomorrow, next month and next year will determine your future. Your thoughts will guide you there.

What you think about the most, you will attract to you. That's the law of attraction at work. So if you are thinking good positive thoughts about your goal, you will attract that to yourself. But always keep this in mind, this law works like a double edge sword. It will lead you to success or it will lead you to failure. It's all about how you use it.

It's all up to you.

A Very Interesting Story

As I mentioned earlier,

Success is the progressive realization of a worthy idea.

If you know why you are doing what you are doing and where you are going, you are a success.

And a person who has no goal, who does not know what they want or know where they are going must be by this definition be unsuccessful.

This is really a simple definition for success. But if it is so simple why are there only a small group of people who are successful? By this definition EVERYONE should be successful but they are not.

You see the problem with most people is they are playing the worlds most unrewarding game and the name of the game is: Follow the Follower.

Many years ago, when the big factory existed in almost every town, they use to blow a big quitting whistle to let everyone know when it was 5 o'clock pm, and time to go home. This whistle was also heard for miles around.

The owner of a jewelry shop would notice how every morning a man would stop and look through the window of his jewelry shop each morning to set his watch. This went on for years. One morning while the owner of the jewelry shop was outside sweeping his part of the sidewalk, the man came by once again, looked through the window of the shop and set his watch.

The owner: "I've noticed that each morning you set your watch according to my big clock here in the shop, Why is that?"

The man: "Well I am the manager down at the big factory. I need to have the correct time. I am responsible for blowing the quitting whistle at 5 o'clock pm.

The owner: „Hmm, I have been setting my clock by the sound of the quitting whistle at 5 o'clock pm at the factory all these years."

Interesting isn't it. Following the follower, without knowing why. The time could have been wrong by as much as 6 months!

Conformity — people acting like everyone else, without knowing why or where they are going. This is what happens when a person goes along with what he thinks is right without checking his references. So if you do nothing else at least check your references. If you are going to follow someone find out if they are going where you want to go.

I would like to share a very interesting story with you about an average young lady in our society.

Now from the time this little girl is born there is only one thing that she can do and that is to begin to think and act like the people around her. That's all she can do. Now right here there is a 95% chance that she is thinking, acting and talking like the wrong group. They may love her and wish that she succeeds, but chances are they do not have the answers she needs to reach fulfillment as a person and to have success. If this is an unhealthy environment that she is raised in, she will never get the answers she needs to success, never learn how to reach into those large pools of ability and genius she has and use them.

Well, now she starts school. The most important thing for a little girl in school is to be liked by the other kids in school. It is at this young age she will follow other kids around, who are the same age, who don't know any more than she does and for the most part they do not have any leadership qualities. She will try to do the hardest thing there is to do and that is to try and please the other kids; to be like someone else to fit into the group. She never learns that all she has to do is just be herself. She will do this in the 1st grade, 2nd grade, 3rd grade, 4th grade, 5th grade and continue this pattern up to the 11th and 12th grade, until it's time to leave school. Year after year developing herself into a composite average of the kids she is hanging around with. Trying to be like them, trying to do the only thing that is impossible for a person to do - be like someone else.

Let's say she finishes school, picks up some general administration skills along the way. Stays in or near her hometown. She is single, not really sure what to do. She's standing at a bus stop, runs into a friend from school who says: "Silvia, what are you up to? She replies: "Nothing" and the friend continues: "Why don't you come down and work where I work? It's a big company that pays very well and lots of benefits." And she does just that. So the chances are great that her first job is based on "random application." She didn't chose the job because that's what she want be. She chose the job because that's what everyone else is doing.

On the job, without thinking about it, the most natural thing in the world to do is for her to look around and see how everyone else is doing their job and do her job the same way. Assuming whats normal for them is normal for her. No reason for this. She doesn't even think about it, she just does it.

She now has before her 50 years; living in the greatest era of all time, one that people have dreamed about for over a thousand of years. It's the era of unlimited possibilities. To be, do or have anything you want. What is she going to do with these 50 golden years? Let's take a close look and find out.

As a rule we know she works around 40 hours a week. Which leaves 72 hours a week when she is neither working or sleeping. 72 free hours each week to do with as she pleases. She is married now, has an apartment, car and here is what she will do with those free 72 hours a week, which is basically what everyone else is doing with their free 72 hours a week - nothing at all.

She with go to work everyday, get off work at the same time every day, drive home, give her husband a kiss and say "I'm tired." Experts have reasoned that people say they are tired because they picked that up from their parents, who picked it up from their parents who may have really put in the hard hours doing hard labor jobs like farm work or construction work many years ago. So today she's just repeating what she heard growing up.

She will have an evening meal and then relax in front of the television. She will sit for 5 or 6 hours viewing those shows aimed at catching her interest. There is nothing wrong with watching television except she's watching people who make an excellent income, who are in pursuit of their dreams and goals.

These people are going after their goals while she sits there with no goal and no plan.

Do not misunderstand me here, I enjoy television too. If there is a good show on that is of interest to me I will watch it. But I also have goals. Visions of things I want to be, do or have and I take action. I have to work at that more if I want to make things happen in my life. So instead of watching television, I love to "tell-a-vision" about my goals and how I will reach them.

Now she will sit there and watch television until she falls asleep, her husband who is a little more practical then she is, will tap her on the shoulder and say "Silvia, it's time for bed, you know you have to get up early in the morning." She understands this and gets up and goes to bed. Next morning she gets up goes to work and will do this all over again. She continues to do this everyday for 20 years or more. She is unhappy with her life, the reason is because she is not doing anything with her life. Instead of taking responsibility for her life, she will blame someone else for her unhappiness. At the end of 40 years she will retire, which surprises her when she realizes she spent so much time doing the same thing all those years. With the advancement in medical science, she will die at age 85 or 90 from complete boredom.

What's the problem? Is there a tragedy here? Not really if that's the way Silvia wants to live her life; our mythical, hypothetical young lady. If she wants to live her life that way she is free to do so. She can do anything with her life she wants.

It's only a terrible tragedy if she's living that way simply because she failed to make a decision. If she's living that way because she is still doing the same thing she did in the first and second grade which is doing what everyone else is doing. It's a tragedy because it means she followed the wrong group of people and did not accomplish any more than they did. She never finds out who she is, never finds out about her abilities and talents. Never learns she can be, do, or have anything she wants in life and that is a pity.

What's needed here? Well I think a checklist is needed. Airplane pilots use a check list before taking off and before landing. They do not trust all the important steps they need to take to memory. Our lives are very important to us, I think we need a checklist to get our lives started. A list that we can use to check ourselves with in the morning and then again before going to bed at night. It's a very important task to get our lives started right. Here is what I think should be on that checklist to help this woman lead a more happy, interesting, exciting and more enjoyable life.

The first thing that she should have on the checklist is "have a goal." A person without a goal is like a ship without compass. Oh, you are moving and you are going somewhere, you just don't know where. Without a goal you have no direction and no purpose. Find yourself a goal. Stay with it and you will get to where you want to be.

The second thing on the checklist is "attitude." It's the most important word in the world. It's your attitude towards the world that reflects the worlds attitude towards you. If you put out hate and arrogance that is what you will get back. Smile and be happy and you get that back. Your environment will match your attitude. Think positive and watch what happens to your surroundings. It's simple yet most people forget it.

Third on the list would be the word "Think." It's the highest function you can perform. Write down your goal on piece of paper and think of ways you can achieve it.

Fourth on the list is the law of Cause and Effect. The rewards we receive in life will reflect the service that we provide. You want to increase your income? Write down ways you can improve on the service you are currently giving. We are all given a life but it is up to us to make something great out of it.

Fifth on the list would be "truthful." You need to be honest with yourself and the people you work for or the people that work for you.

Sixth is "Research and Development." Nobody wants to work for a company that does not invest in its own future. Investing money and finding ways to do things better is how the company survives. Your job at the company where you work exists because your company is constantly finding ways to grow. And if the company doesn't grow you will lose your job. You have seen this happen, probably even experienced it yourself.

Now, how much money have you invested in yourself? How much money did you spend last year to make yourself smarter this year?

How much money are you investing in yourself right now so you can be smarter next year than you are now? What are you doing to help you love a little more and hate a little less. How much money are you putting back into yourself and your future? It's something to think about.

And finally, the seventh thing on the list, always remember and never forget: "We become what we think about most of the time." That is why thinking is so important and why you should have a goal. We become what we think about the most. Basic, simple and true.

If we want to become something we need individual goals, individual thinking, individual action and NEVER conform to the big group. We must love them, help them, and serve them because our success will depend on our ability to do these things. But never lose our own individuality, our identity by following the wrong group of people. If you want to follow someone that's ok but be selective. Choose from the group of the highly successful people.

You only live once, but if you do it right, once is enough.

Paradigm Shift

There's only one corner of the universe you can be certain of improving, and that's your own self. Aldous Huxley

In order to change your life, you are going to have to change your way of thinking. That means you are going to have to change your paradigm. Although "paradigm" has become a buzz word in the 21st century not many people can tell you what a paradigm is.

Everything you know how to do now you learned it by constantly repeating it. Take for example tying your shoes. Watch a little kid trying to tie up their shoes. They try to loop the string around and it doesn't work. But they keep trying and after awhile those little fingers finally get it and they can tie their shoes. You and I can tie up our shoes while having a conversation with someone or while watching TV. We don't even have to look at our shoes and really don't give the issue much thought because we have done it so often. That's a habit.

Now look at your morning routine. You get up wash your face, go make coffee, shower and get dressed. You stand and put your pants on right leg first. If you were to start with your left leg first you would probably fall on the floor. These are things you do without thinking about them. They are your habits. Put these habits together in a group, that's your paradigm.

Now you want to make changes in your life. You want to get up early in the morning and be a part of the 6 am morning club, write down your goals and how you can do things better. That's a new habit. So you have to change or break your current paradigm. That's the paradigm shift.

Paradigms are formed through repetition and that's exactly how we change them. Paradigms control the results in our lives. To ignore the power of paradigms is to put yourself at risk when exploring the future. And I know I don't want to put myself at risk.

In times of change the learners will inherit the earth, while the learned will find themselves beautifully equipped to deal with a world that no longer exists. Eric Hoffer

To make changes in your life and to change a paradigm you have to learn to take control your mind. To control your mind its helpful to know how your mind works.

So, here's the deal; you and I think in pictures. And very very few people have an image when it comes to the mind. If I say to to you the word "bird" you do not see the letters b...i...r...d in your mind, instead you see the picture of a bird.

Now let me show you how fast I can change the pictures in your mind...

go to your car, go to your clothes closet, go to your kitchen, your refrigerator, go to your bedroom and now go to your front door. Did you see how fast you were flipping pictures? Ok now go to your mind. And there is no picture. That's where the problem begins. So when we think of the mind most people think of the brain. Mind is movement, But the brain is not your mind. Your brain is part of your body. The mind uses the brain, it activates brain cells to get things done and is a storage place for information. The brain can not think but you think with the brain. Now to explain that a little further and clearer, I read once where they had the brain from Albert Einstein put away safely in a jar somewhere in Pennsylvania but it's not doing anybody any good because Albert is not with it.

You use your brain. Just like you use your hands or your feet. You need to activate brain cells and provide it with a picture of the mind so you can control it better. So now all you need is a picture of the mind.

In 1934, Dr. Thurmond Fleet, from San Antonio, Texas, who was very involved in the healing arts said we have a serious problem here. We are not going to see any health until we start treating the whole person. All we doing now is treating symptoms. The body is the expression of the disease, the disease is inside. And that's just what it is "dis ease". To eliminate the disease, we have to go to the cause of it. You see, we live on 3 levels of understanding; 1) we are spiritual beings, 2) we have an intellect and 3) we live in a physical body. if there is a problem with a person then all 3 levels have been affected, the spiritual, the intellect and the body. We have to treat the whole person and to do this we have to have an image to work with and he created a picture of the mind and the body.

The drawing you see here is the stick person of the mind and body. It's a simple drawing but it is incredibly powerful. Wherever I go to talk and teach, I take this drawing with me. Top business people and companies around the world are familiar with this picture of the mind. This is a picture of my mind. It is a picture of your mind. You will hear me often say, "I do not know what other people are thinking however I do know how they are thinking"

and it based on this photo of the mind from Dr. Thurmond Fleet.

If you are around me I will be watching your body language based on this picture and that is going to tell me what's going inside of you. We hide nothing. Everything that happens on the inside shows up on the outside.

Now there are two parts to the mind. The conscious and the subconscious. The conscious is referred to as the intellectual mind. The subconscious is called the universal or emotional mind. Now both of these parts function totally differently.

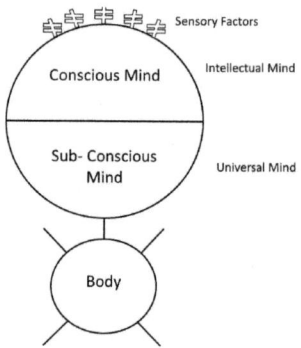

The conscious mind is the thinking mind. It is here that we can accept or reject anything. Those "Sensory Factors" are the ability to see, hear, smell, taste and touch. Let's say you are watching the news and you get information that the economy is going down. That information came in over your Sensory Factors. But whether you believe that is totally up to you. Are you aware that during the Great Depression of the 1930's there were people who made millions of dollars? The economy was not bad for everyone. It went up for some, mainly because they refused to accept it and had a lot more belief in themselves and their business projects. This means that we are in control. As

84

information comes in you have to ask yourself this question, is the information that's coming in right now aligned with my purpose and can it help me reach my goals? If it is then you accept it and use it. If it is not you reject it. And just because everyone else is doing it is not a good enough reason for you to do it. If you want to be, do and have more, you will not get it doing what everyone else is doing. So if the masses are going in one direction and one or two successful people are going in the other direction and you are not sure what to do, follow the one or two. But that's how the conscious mind works, it accepts or rejects.

Now the subconscious mind cannot do that. The subconscious mind will accept anything you give to it. It has no ability to reject. It just simply accepts. And here is something else you need to know about the subconscious mind, it can not tell the difference between what's real and what's imagined. Anyone from the medical field will tell you that "placebos" are commonly used, although many can not tell you where the word comes from. The word "placebo" comes from the Latin verb "to please". A medical professional can give a person a sugar pill or a yellow M&M candy and tell them that it will stop all pain immediately or that this will put you right to sleep. And just as quick as a snap, the pain is gone or they fall asleep. A nurse can take a syringe, push a little bit of the liquid out of it, and say this will help you sleep. She will fix the arm and give them a shot and the person is out for the next for 12 hours.

Why? Because the nurse told them that they were going to be out of it for 12 hours. That this is very powerful medicine for putting you to sleep. Do you know what was really in it? Nothing but distilled water. How does that happen? Well it's the idea. The conscious mind is set aside. They are not thinking. The subconscious mind accepts and believes what the medical professional tells them.

The idea is placed in the subconscious mind and person believes it as fact and it is expressed through the body. This is happening all the time.

Now mentally take yourself back to the time when you were a baby. When you were born you had no conscious factors.

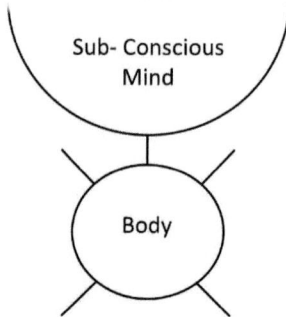

Your subconscious was wide open. People around you were saying and doing things. Eating certain types of food, the way they talked, the way they worked and how they got along with other people and it all went straight to your subconscious mind. This repetition of an idea becomes fixed and planted in your head.

There is in fact a chain of events that occur through us as individuals and most of us don't even know its going on. It's really simple too.

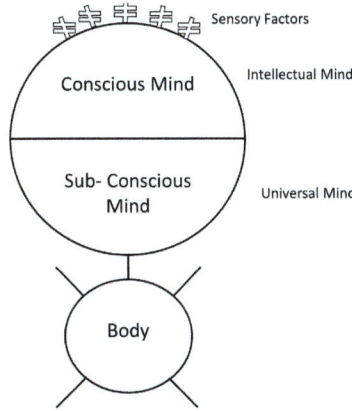

1) Sensory Factors are your antennas for: smell, taste, touch, hearing and seeing.

2) You think in your conscious mind. You make a decision to accept or not the things your Sensory Factors experience.

3) This gets passed to your subconscious mind as what you believe.

4) Which your body expresses. It brings about the changes in your physical world and subsequently the results you get.

When I use this diagram on myself, I tend to visualize my own head; my eyes are the middle point. Everything above my eyes is conscious and everything below is subconscious.

You think in your conscious mind, your subconscious mind has no choice but to accept it and the results are seen around you. So if you are consistently thinking about how little money you have, how lonely you are, that you are not a good person or that you are a dumb person who can't learn anything then that's what getting passed down to your subconscious mind and that's the results you get. Remember what I said earlier...

You become what you think about

This diagram shows you how that works. To take control of your life you first need to take control of your thinking.

Here is the challenge. Your senses act like antenna that feed information to your conscious mind and they allow you to check out the world around you. To change the paradigm you need the ability to be able to ignore what's going on around you and originate your own thoughts.

For example, if you are listening to the news everyday, as most people do, you constantly hear and see reports on how bad the economy is. The news media reports mostly negativity anyway. Informative? Yes, but the negativity is there. As you continue to listen and watch the news, absorbing this negativity, eventually that becomes your belief and you begin to talk about it with your friends and everyone else; about how bad the economy is. The basic thought becomes, "That idea will not work, because the economy is bad." Are you aware that even in a "bad economy" there are people who are making millions! They don't believe in a bad economy. They make their own economy. They believe in what they are doing, and that they can provide a service to others.

You can do the same. If your sensory factors are giving you information, you have the ability to replace those thoughts. You may think you are alone, but you are not. There are people out there who are on your side. With the thoughts of knowing that you are surrounded by loving friends and with people who can help you move forward, this is what will get passed to your subconscious (remember it doesn't have a choice) and it will lead to you being able to change your paradigm and begin getting great results.

Purpose, Vision, Goals

"What a different story people would have to tell if they would adopt a definite purpose and stand by that purpose until it had time to become an all-consuming purpose."

Napoleon Hill, Laws of Success

Why are you here? Or, in relationship to your job, a better question might be "Why are you doing what you are doing?." If your reason is because "Well, everyone has to work and that's why I do it" or "I have to pay the rent and other bills", that's not good enough. We all have unlimited potential and I simply do not believe we are here just to work jobs we do not enjoy, to pay rent, mortgage and a list of other bills because that's what everyone does and then at the end of the week go party, drink beer and cocktails. There is more to life than that.

It doesn't matter how you think you arrived here on this planet or under whose direction - the fact remains that each of us has specific talents, gifts and the unlimited power to learn anything.

As you go through life you discover there are things you are good at, you feel good and comfortable when you do them, like you were born to do it. Other times new experiences bring new discoveries to you. As you travel and experience life, you gain new interests and desires.

And it's from these specific talents, gifts, new experiences, new interests and desires that you are able to define and determine your definite purpose, the reason why you are here. Yes, knowing your "purpose" is very serious business.

Not being able to to determine your definite purpose, makes life

90

confusing. It's like working with a broken compass. You may think you are going North, but you are not. You are not sure in which direction you are going, you're wandering around, never arriving at the place where you want to be.

Without knowing why you are here, you wander through life, never quite feeling that you're "in the flow." I say then that it is very important that you recognize what it is you are good at doing. What is that thing that you really love to do? **Your purpose in this lifetime is to do the thing that you love.**

People will tell you that they already know what they are good at doing, and what they love to do the most, but they say they can never earn money doing it. Where did they get that idea? You can earn money at ANYTHING. Once you know your purpose, you will not have to think so hard on how to earn money. It will come to you. When you are going in the right direction, everything will fall in place.

The key to your life is not to settle for something "safe" that will bring you money. The key is to do that thing that you really love. Fall in love with an idea. That's your life! That's your purpose.

You see, when you fall in love with an idea you are in harmony with it. That's what you think about all the time. It dictates the vibration of your body and moves you into action. This idea that you are in harmony with yourself about what you want to do with your life will push you out of bed in the morning before your alarm clock goes off. You are full of energy to do this thing that you love so much.

Your purpose also gives meaning to WHY you are here on the planet. Why you are doing what you are doing. So when a person falls in love with an idea, their conscious and subconscious are working together and in harmony; they're in sync. By staying in harmony and focusing on your goal and believing in yourself is how you get past the negatives. Those negative images bring about fear and in many cases that's the reason why people fail. The constant attention on the negative keeps people from moving in the direction that they really want to go.

You have had failure in your life. I've had failure in my life. When we fail its not a fault issue - we simply were not in harmony with what we were trying to do. I remember when growing up, one summer I wanted to take guitar lessons. I was given an electric guitar, amplifier and all. The guitar lessons were not my thing. I failed at learning to play the guitar. Two months later (american) football practice started up and I had great fun. I trained hard and was successful with playing football for a few years. What happened? Well I had an interest learning to play the guitar, but I was not in harmony with it. I was not sleeping, eating and thinking about the guitar 24 hours a day, 7 days a week. But when it came to football I was in harmony with that. I would play football with friends on the playground, watch the college games on Saturday and the professional games on Sunday. By Monday morning I was ready to go to practice. And practice was hard but I loved it. It all worked because I was in harmony with that. That was my purpose, that was what I really wanted to do.

So the question will always be, what do you want? What is it that you truly love to do?

You must realize and recognize the unique gift of YOU. You can be, do or have anything you want. When you start focusing on the things you want, you put yourself in harmony with those things. And that's when you begin to make things happen because you know your purpose.

Also remember, you are not on this planet to live someone else's dream. It's all about YOU and what you love to do. So when you believe you have found your purpose, do not let the opinions of other people change your mind. Don't let other people tell you in which direction you should go with your life.

Here's a great example of what I mean. I have always had an interest in photography but never had the time to focus on it. Finally after making some changes and adjustments in my life, I had time to learn photography. I went out a bought a very nice camera and started taking pictures. I was out on a regular basis, taking photos and teaching myself along the way. The more photos I took the better I would get (and that is really key to successful photography). I had some really great shots. I wanted to know more. I had friends and knew people who were photographers and thought that would be a great place to start. But to my surprise, no one wanted to teach me or share their information. It's hard sometimes when you want to do something but can't find the help you need. Sometimes people just give up. But I did not, I just kept practicing and searching for some good and useful information.

Eventually, I did get in contact with one professional photographer. I was even on location as he was doing a themed photo shooting session with models. When time allowed it we talked and I was able to explain what I had already learned. I also had some really simple but important questions about equipment and setting up a location that I needed answers to. I even brought some of my great shots along to show off. After looking at my photos and everything, he replied with the following:

"I am a photographer and I am very good at what I do. I have been doing this for years. And here's the the thing; I was born to do this. I can look at a scene and just know how to set it up. This is in my blood. And that's something that not everyone can do."

On my way home I was thinking, ok, I was not born to do this. Maybe I am a little out of my leauge on this one. But a moment later I thought: Why am I letting him steal my dream?! This is my DREAM and my HOBBY! I know can do this.

I did continue my search and found a great teacher with some wonderful tips to share. And if by chance you're looking for a career change and photography is the way you want to go, here are a few things to keep in mind: 1. Age does not matter. The question is, how bad do you really want it? 2. This guy was not „born" to be a photographer. What happend was this, at a very early age, maybe between 8 – 12 years old, someone gave him a camera and he fell in love with it. He spent all of his free time with it. And the more time he spent learning how to use his camera, the better he got. Now he's over 40 years old, and has been doing this so long he, feels he was born to do this. What he really had was:

Direction, Dedication, Determination, Discipline

If you apply this to what you are doing, no matter what it is, you too will be successful at it. Do it long enough, you will also have a feeling that you were born to do it.

3. Best tip I ever recieved, "People know cars don't drive themselves, computers don't write novels by themselves and that Rembrandt's brushes didn't paint by themselves. So why do some otherwise intelligent people think cameras drive around and make pictures all by themselves? The camera doesn't make a bit of difference. All of them can record what you are seeing. But, you have to SEE."

I see a lot of beauty and I photograph that. My photos make it to promotion material, magazines, and online blogs.

I am not trying to give a photography class here, but my main point is this, if I had listened to this guy I would have given up on my dream, my hobby. Don't let people tell you can't be something. Don't let them talk you out of your dream. You can be anything you want.

Here is want I know to be true. I have done some traveling around the world and have visited some nice countries. Many times I have seen newspaper headlines, magazine articles or watched a TV show were a woman has given birth to a wonderful baby boy or baby girl. I have never heard anyone say, nor have I read an article that says a little baby lawyer, doctor, singer, actor or film director was born. However I have read obituaries where a doctor, singer, actor or film director has passed away. My logical conclusion is this: if they were not born so but can die so, that means that somewhere after birth a person can make a decision to become something and if they take action and believe in themselves, they will become what they think about the most. So find your purpose, that thing you truly enjoy doing no matter what.

Purpose to Vision. Vision to Goal.

Once you know what your purpose is, how do you go about expressing it? You do that by creating and maintaining a vision.

I truly like that what Van Gough once said, "I dream my painting and then I paint my dream." What a powerful statement. Van Gough knew his purpose in life.

His vision was a series of paintings, each one uniquely different from the other. The way he put his vision on the canvas was through a series of short term goals.

Here is great way to show you how to lock in on your vision and set a course to make sure you get there.

I like to travel, and I enjoy weekend trips. However a busy schedule didn't always allow time for them. But when I found out that a music artist I really liked would be doing a concert in Basel, Switzerland, I figured that would be a great time for a weekend trip. At the time I was living in Darmstadt, Germany which is just outside of Frankfurt. And since Basel is only about 3 hours from Frankfurt by car, I thought it would be cool to drive down to Basel for the concert. An added plus would be I could enjoy the scenery along the way. To start, I would pick up a rental car in Frankfurt. Now, to take this trip some planning would have to take place. As I begin to organize my trip it looked like this:

My purpose was to go to a concert. My vision was to drive to Basel and enjoy the concert. My course plan, a layout that would keep me on track and headed in the right direction was: Frankfurt - Heidelberg - Strasbourg - Basel.

So when I got in the car and started my trip, my first stop was Heidelberg. That was the only thing I was thinking of. If I missed getting to Heidelberg then I knew I would not make it to Basel and would not make it to the concert. Now, I didn't have to go directly into Heidelberg, but I did have to go in that general direction. But Heidelberg was a sign that I was on the right course. So, Heidelberg was first on my list, that was my GOAL. After I reached Heidelberg, the next stop would be Strasbourg in order to reach Basel.

I listen to people tell me about their dreams and no matter how they try, they can't seem to make it work. What I have come to learn is that in most cases they're looking for Basel while they are still in Frankfurt. It's great to have Basel as a goal, but you have to set a course and find out what your first stop is. If you do not figure out that your first goal is to get to Heidelberg, it's just going to be difficult getting to Basel. You have to plot your course first. And once you do, you stay active, stay focused and always make progressive steps to get to where you want to go. Always be aware. Sometimes you may have to take a small detour, but never forget what your goal is.

Sometimes after following their dreams for a long period of time, people seem to feel like they just will never get there. They keep driving but never reach their true destination.

I want you to take a moment and imagine that you are in Frankfurt and your goal is to reach Basel. You are in a big rush, you grab all your stuff. You start driving. You realize you need coffee so you stop for coffee. You hop back in your car and start driving again and then...suddenly there is sign that says Cologne 220 km!?

97

And you're thinking, "Wait, I am going to Basel, Switzerland. Cologne is in the opposite direction."

You are somewhat confused and a little worried but you continue to drive in the same direction. An hour goes by and then you see the next sign...Cologne 102 km.

You are getting closer to Cologne. You are now really worried. "How could this be happening?". Now, do you still keep driving in the wrong direction?

Of course not! In a real life situation you would not keep driving this route. As soon as you found out you were going in the wrong direction, you would be looking for an exit. And if it was one of those safe situations where you are the only car on the road and you missed your exit, some of you would hit the brakes and back up to take your exit or even make an illegal U-turn. Why? Because it's important you start going in the right direction NOW. And you remind yourself "I've been going in the wrong direction now for 2 hours!

Why is it that when you are on the road and traveling in the wrong direction you stop and turn around immediately but when it comes down to your life, when it comes to changing the direction of your vision, you keep going in the wrong direction, *even when you know you are going in the wrong direction?*

The key thing to remember here is watch the "street signs."

It's those little things that happen on day to day intervals; your intuition. The signals you get along way that let you know that something you maybe doing is not going to help you with your purpose.

But do not let bumping up against a brick wall or a little resistance stop you. You will just have to change your strategy. Sometimes it may take a little longer that expected. You know it should take you 3 hours to drive from Frankfurt to Basel, but no one told you about the road construction work that creates a traffic jam where sit for an hour or the 45 minute detour you have to take. Just relax and figure out what's the first goal in your vision. A little resistance is good. It helps you grow and raise your level of awareness. Just take action.

It's important to to find and know your purpose. I believe everyone on the planet has a reason for being here. You have to take the time to explore and find out what it is.

There is so much more to life that just working a 9 to 5 job and doing something you know you do not like just to pay a list of bills. You got to take time and find your purpose. You should be doing that thing you truly love to do.

And when you find your purpose, just how ambitious are you? How much do you really want it? What are you willing to sacrifice or endure in order to get yourself headed in the right direction? Even if you find something comes easy to you, you must still work on ways of making yourself better. Are you willing to make the sacrifices in order to turn your goals into reality?

And now a little something about sacrifice.

There is a common misunderstanding out there that "sacrifice" means you are losing something. You are not losing here. When you sacrifice you are giving up something on a lower level in order to get something on a higher level. You are raising your level of awareness, so you can do a better job of helping yourself and others.

**You can't get to the top of the ladder
unless you leave the bottom.**

This is true in every part of life. Think of the person who is looking for a new relationship, but still are holding on to the old one. Look at the people starting diet programs who can't give up the doughnuts and bagel with cream cheese for breakfast. Many people have lost jobs, because of companies reducing their staff, and are out there looking for a new job but they still have the old negative emotional baggage from the last job fixed in their minds.

So, what are you willing to sacrifice to improve your quality of life, and be able to do the things that you love to do? As a guideline I will tell you this, you do not have to violate the rights of others to improve your life. You do not have to have to endanger your life or the lives of the people around you. You do not have to give up your health.

But you will have to give up something that will help you make your dreams come true. Like stop eating doughnuts and bagels for breakfast and take on a fitness routine to improve your health. You may have to deal with a temporary money crunch until your idea is up and running. You can also take the time to spend a couple a nights a week to get that extra training and certification you may need for a promotion or a better job.

It all comes down to this:

Find your purpose, that one thing you enjoy doing more than

anything else.

Build your vision. Set your goals.

Believe in yourself. Take action.

The 30-Day Secret
Your Challenge for 30 Days of Growth

Scientists have suggested that with a little willpower it takes about 30 days for a person to form a new habit. As with mastering anything new, it is the act of starting and getting beyond that stage where everything feels awkward. That's 80% of the battle. This is precisely why it's important to make small, positive changes every day over the course of at least a 30 day period.

The 30 Day secret is also how the 30 day money back guarantee works. You buy an item and you get a 30 day money back guarantee. The logic behind the guarantee is if you use the product regularly, say for 30 days, it becomes part of your new habit and you will want to keep the product. This happens because you have developed a new habit of using that item.

So now it's time to develop new habits to get your life going in a new direction.

Trying to change everything all at once will set you up for failure. So here is what you need to do. You start with some small steps first. You pick one new habit and slowly make it a part of your day and week. The more you use it the more it becomes a part of you. Soon you will be amazed and excited about how you can make positive changes to your life.

The simple act of getting started and doing something will give you the momentum you need. Soon you'll find yourself having a positive spiral of changes – one building on the other.

Listed on the following pages you will find 25 challenges to be accomplished over the course of 30 days. If carried out with an honest desire to change, each of them has the potential to make a major impact on your life. Again, the idea here is not to try to change everything at once. Read through the list and start by picking one or two challenges and commit to making them a part of your daily routine for the next 30 days. Then once you feel comfortable with these habits, you take the next step and add a new challenge to your daily routine the following month.

Always, use daily and repeat often.

1. TO CHANGE YOUR LIFE
YOU HAVE TO CHANGE YOUR LIFE

Always remember this. It sounds like a play on words. Yet this is so basic and so powerful.

"The primary reason for failure is that people do not develop new plans to replace those plans that didn't work." (Napoleon Hill)

If you are not getting the results you are looking for, then you need a new strategy. I will let you in on a little secret, successful people are not people without problems. Successful people are people who have learned how to find solutions for their problems.

Taking responsibility for your actions is important. In every study of successful people, the acceptance of personal responsibility seems to be the starting point. Before that, nothing happens. After you accept complete responsibility, your whole life begins to change.

When I was starting over with my life, that was my first step, to constantly remind myself that I am responsible for my life.

2. WRITE IT DOWN

You need to start doing this right now. Go out and buy a journal or staple some blank pages together and make your own. Many great people, past and present have expressed how important it is to write things down. So if you want to model the success of successful people, do as they do, write things down.

If you want to achieve something in your life like, being a musician, a writer, actor, doctor, a great business person, get better grades in school or excel in sports or whatever it may be, you need to write it down and be specific. Go into detail about this thing you are going to do.

You need to find the time to make a list of your dreams and goals and maintain that list throughout your life. Write down the things you want, check off the things you have achieved and add your new goals and dreams to the list.

Here is how you get started. Make your list by putting the things you want in categories:

Body & Health

Work & Career

Relationships

Money

Personal desires

Material things

Now just take the time to add the things you want to have to your list. When you know what you want you can begin to focus more on it. This will help you define the direction you need to take to make things happen.

You also need to write about yourself and your life. What are you thinking right now? Write it down. You want to get rid of that extra weight? Start writing down what you eat and when. You will be surprised. Only when you see and understand your eating style can you begin to make changes to improve it.

Still not sure what to write about? Then write about this:

Monday: Thanksgiving
There are many things to be thankful for. From the past week list 3 things.

Tuesday: Terrific Times
Think about one of the most wonderful experiences in your life.

Wednesday: Future Fantastic
Spend a few moments writing about your life in the future.

Thursday: Dear...
Write about the person who is important to you and why. You do not have to send them the note. This is a reminder to yourself that you do have great people around you.

Friday: Reviewing The Situation
Think back over the past seven days and make a note of 3 things that went really well for you. Whether it's about finding great parking space or a job opportunity.

3. IMPROVE YOUR SELF TALK

When was last time you told yourself something like: "I can't handle it any more", or "How could I be so stupid" or "I will never be able to _____ " ? (I will let you fill in the blank). Have you noticed that sometimes when you want to do something you have never done before, the first person to talk you out of it is yourself?

"Self-talk" refers to the dialogue that goes on inside your head – the way you communicate with yourself. We all have this. This internal dialogue affects how you feel about yourself, your colleagues, your job, and your life. The good news is that although you may not be able to control everything that happens, you can control the way you think about and react to those situations. Positive self-talk can encourage you, relieve stress, and improve your self-image. Negative self-talk, on the other hand, increases stress, chips away at self-esteem, and can cause you to overreact.

Think of your positive and negative self-talk as the voices of two different people. One is supportive, caring and encouraging. The other complains frequently, puts you down, and is quick to find the worst in everything. Who would you rather listen to?

The thing with negative self-talk is this: Our thoughts race at a hundred miles an hour, jumping uncontrollably from one self-diminishing thought to the next without consciously registering as such. Think about it. If someone else was putting you down the way you put down yourself, your senses would immediately awaken, and you would probably defend yourself. However, with negative self-talk, there is no such self-defense mechanism. All this negativity is blindly absorbed and is therefore all the more toxic to our lives and particularly the relationship we have with ourselves.

This is clearly not the road to travel in order to be the most flourishing, lovely, and sparkling versions of ourselves, now is it? Think about it; you would probably never talk to your best friend the way you often talk to yourself, because you know that it would probably affect them negatively. This brings me to my first suggested way to stop that ugly negative self-talk:

1) Don't say anything to yourself that you wouldn't say to your best friend. If you catch yourself on a self-depreciating rant, check in with yourself and ask, "Would I say this to _____?" If the answer is "no," then you certainly don't deserve to be spoken to in that way either. Don't let these insults pass without defending yourself against your own negative and grumpy voice.

2) Write out the insult you just said to yourself. Seeing it on a piece of paper will make it more obvious to you how self-depreciating your thoughts really are. When you think something like, "I am so dumb," it likely passes through your mind so swiftly, you don't have a chance to even register it. So many of us are so used to this kind of talk that we literally have to slow ourselves down and re-register what we are actually saying to ourselves. Writing it out is a great way to slow down and see the absurdity in your own negative self-talk.

3) Take a break from social media. Studies show that social media increases self-criticism. Instead, spend some time tuning in to yourself and how you feel about and see your own life through your own eyes. Listen. Pay attention to your own thoughts. Say something nice to yourself. Be with yourself, and get clear on what you actually think and feel about who you are. This is difficult for so many of us, but if you cannot be with yourself, how do you expect anyone else to be with you? If you speak to yourself disrespectfully or even flat-out rudely, how do you expect anyone else to treat you differently? By elevating your self-treatment to a standard that aligns with your value

system, your environment will follow suite. That's the law of attraction.

4) Formulate an intention that originates from your heart about the way you want to speak with yourself and hence, feel about yourself. The only rule is that your intention has to be affirmative (formulate your sentences using "do" instead of "don't," etc.), written in the first person, and in the present tense. Pour all your creativity, playfulness, and personal quirkiness into this note, so that it truly feels like YOU. Then, put it up somewhere where you will see it daily or perhaps exactly there, where most of your negative self-talk tends to happen.

4. ESTABLISH A DAILY MEDITATION PRACTICE

Taking into consideration that there are many different types of meditation techniques available, I will give you a simple and easy to understand technique. Yes, meditation works and it's very effective but it's also helpful to know the behind the scenes details of "why" meditation works so well to calm your mind and body.

A great, simple breathing exercise for calming both the nervous system and the overworked mind is a timed breath where the exhale is longer than the inhale. When your exhale is even a few counts longer than your inhale, the vagus nerve (running from the neck down through the diaphragm) sends a signal to your brain to turn up your parasympathetic nervous system and turn down your sympathetic nervous system.

The sympathetics command your fight or flight response, and when they fire, your heart rate and your breathing speed up, and stress hormones like cortisol start pumping through your bloodstream, preparing your body to face a threat. If the threat is, "A lion is chasing me and I need to run away," this is helpful. If the threat is, "I am late to work" or, "I'm so upset with _____ ," this is not particularly helpful, and in fact it can be damaging – when cortisol is elevated for too long or too frequently it disturbs all the hormonal systems of the body.

The parasympathetics, on the other hand, control your rest, relax, and digest response. When the parasympathetic system is dominant, your breathing slows, your heart rate drops, your blood pressure lowers as the blood vessels relax, and your body is put into a state of calm and healing.

Putting your body in a parasympathetic state is easy. Pick a count for your inhale and a count for your exhale that is a little longer. I like starting with 2 counts in, and 4 counts out, with a one count pause at the top of the inhale and a one count pause at the bottom of the exhale.

Step by step instructions:

To begin, sit still and tall somewhere comfortable. Close your eyes and being breathing through your nose.

Then, inhale for a count of two… hold the breath in for a count of one… exhale gently, counting out for four… and finish by holding the breath out for a count of one. Keep your breathing even and smooth.

If the 2-4 count feels too short try increasing the breath lengths to 4 in and 6 out, or 6 in and 8 out, and so on. But if longer breaths create any anxiety there is no need to push yourself.

The most important thing is that the exhale is longer than the inhale, not the absolute length of the breath.

Set a timer and breathe this way for at least five minutes! You will see a difference in your mood.

5. FORGET ABOUT LUCK

Whatever happens in your life - good or bad, doesn't come by way of luck, lack of luck, karma or sins of your forefathers. What happens in your life is up to you and the choices you make. It's about how hard are you willing to work for it.

"It is our choices, Harry, that show what we truly are, far more than our abilities." —
   Albus Dumbledore in Harry Potter & the Chamber of Secrets

I am reminded of an interview done with a professional golfer. The golfer won the three day tournament by making fantastic putting shots. During the interview a reporter asked "You had fantastic luck with all of your putting shots, how can you explain that?" The reply from the professional golfer was "Well, it seems the harder I practice, the luckier I get."

So it stands to reason that if you know what you want and willing to take the time to work towards that goal, you will find yourself having that "luck" that so many other people have.

6. YOU CAN LEARN ANYTHING

You can learn anything you need to learn to accomplish any goal you can set for yourself. No one is smarter than you and no one is better than you. All business skills, sales skills and moneymaking skills are learnable. Everyone who is good in any area today was once poor in that area. The top people in every field were at one time not even in that field and didn't even know that that field existed. And what hundreds of thousands of other people have done, you can do as well. Learn and practice one new skill every day. Self-reliance is a vital key to living a healthy, productive life. To be self-reliant one must master a basic set of skills, more or less making them a jack of all trades. Contrary to what you may have learned in school, a jack of all trades is far more equipped to deal with life than a specialized master of only one. And besides, learning new skills is fun.

7. THE ART OF GRATITUDE

Do you want more from your life? More happiness? Better health? Deeper relationships? Increased productivity?

You have something good going on in your life right now. We all do. Gratitude is the art of being grateful for those good things that are happening right now for you. Be thankful for what you now have and you open up the the doors to being able to attract more good things into your life.

Yes, some days it can be challenging for us to find things to be grateful for. And while stress can trigger past or future focus, gratitude keeps you in the present.

When you focus your attention on being thankful for being, doing, having, letting go of, you are connecting with the present moment and attracting more of the good stuff to your life. By being thankful for good things that you have in your life, you create more positive thoughts that are set in gratitude and you attract even more positive experiences to be grateful for.

What are some of the of the things you could be thankful for? You can be thankful for your family, friends, relationships and the place where you are living right now. You can be thankful for your life, your health, the air you breath, the sun, the water you drink and the food you eat. You can be thankful for the plants, trees, flowers, the moon, and the stars. You didn't go to sleep hungry last night. You didn't go to sleep outside. You had a choice of what clothes to wear this morning. You hardly broke a sweat today. You didn't spend a minute in fear. You have access to clean drinking water. You have access to medical care. You have access to the Internet. You can read. And there are so many other things that are in your life and that our beautiful planet has to offer. Some might say you are incredibly wealthy, so remember to be grateful for all the things you do have.

Start noticing how wealthy you are right now. Henry David Thoreau once said, "Wealth is the ability to fully experience life." Even when times are tough, it's always important to keep things in perspective.

There are many ways to practice gratitude. A common method to develop the practice of gratitude is to keep a gratitude journal. This exercise takes only 5 minutes of your time.

When you wake up in the morning write down five things for

which you are grateful. Also, write down "*why*" you are thankful for the things and people in your life.

Or, before you go to bed at night, take 5 minutes and go through your day and write down five things that you are thankful for.

You can also do this twice a day, mornings when you get up and at night before you go to bed.

8. GRATITUDE ROCK

Life challenges us day after day. We have so many great things happening to us in our lives that we forget how good our life really is. The gratitude rock is a great reminder. I started the practice back in 2009 and I have had great success with my gratitude rock. It has been a constant reminder to be thankful for what I have and it has turned into great habit that I use everyday.

First thing you need to do is find a small smooth stone. You can visit a nearby river or stream, beach or park. There are some small shops that have small stones in many different shapes and colors. You are looking for something thats small, smooth and feels good in your hand. A stone that you can carry with you wherever you go.

Now take your gratitude stone and place it where you can see. Even better, put in a place where you will be reminded to take it with you no matter where you go. Place it by your keys or even on your key ring. I started out carrying my gratitude rock in the same pocket as my mobile phone. Each time I use my phone, I touch my gratitude rock and I am instantly reminded to think of the things that I am thankful for. Other times when sitting in a waiting room somewhere, because of its smoothness, I would hold it in my hand; massage my palm and list at least ten things that I was thankful for. I still carry my gratitude rock with me. I never leave the house without it.

Think back, about your day, your life and about all the good things that have happened to you. Good things happen to all of us, it's just a matter of taking the time to remind ourselves of those wonderful things. Once you have found that for which you are thankful for, say the following: "*Thank you for ...*" and list the people, places or things in your life that you are thankful for. That's all you have to do!

ALWAYS look for the best thing that has happened and be thankful for that. The power of gratitude is great. Only when you are thankful for what you have can you begin to receive more of it and many other things as well.

So now EVERYDAY take the time to be thankful.

9. CREATE YOUR OWN VISION BOARD

Your brain will work tirelessly to achieve the statements you give your subconscious mind. And when those statements and affirmations are connected to images of your goals, you are destined to achieve them!

Creating a vision board is probably one of the most valuable visualization tools available to you. This powerful tool serves as your image of the future - YOUR FUTURE. And it is a tangible representation of where you are going. It represents your dreams, your goals, and your ideal life.

Because your mind responds strongly to visual stimulation, by representing your goals with pictures and images you will actually strengthen and stimulate your emotions. Your emotions are the vibrational energy that activates the Law of Attraction. There is a saying that goes "A picture is worth a thousand words," and that is what it's all about here. You have a goal and now you associate that goal with a picture.

First, start looking for pictures that represent or symbolize the experiences, feelings, and possessions you want to attract into your life, and place them on your board. You should have some fun and enjoy yourself while doing this. Use photographs, magazine cutouts, pictures from the Internet, whatever inspires you. Be creative. Include not only pictures, but anything that speaks to you.

Consider including a picture of yourself. If you do, choose one that was taken in a happy moment. You will also want to post your affirmations, inspirational words, quotations, and thoughts here. Choose words and images that inspire you and make you feel good.

You can use your vision board to show your goals and dreams in all areas of your life, or in just one specific area that you are focusing on. Keep it neat, and be selective about what you place on your vision board. Use only the words and images that best represent your purpose, your ideal future, and words that inspire positive emotions in you. There is beauty in simplicity and clarity. Too many images and too much information will be distracting and harder to focus on.

Keep your vision board next to your bed. It's the last thing you see before going to bed and the first thing you see in the morning. Take a picture of your vision board and use it as wallpaper on your computer or mobile telephone. The more time you spend with your vision board the better. Spend time each morning and evening, also during the day, visualizing, affirming, believing, and internalizing your goals.

The time you spend visualizing in the evening just before bed is especially powerful. The thoughts and images that are present in your mind during the last forty-five minutes before going to sleep are the ones that will replay themselves repeatedly in your subconscious mind through out the night, and the thoughts and images that you begin each day with will help you to create a vibrational match for the future you desire.

As some time goes by and your dreams begin to manifest, look at those images that represent your achievements, and feel gratitude for how well the law of attraction is working in your life. Acknowledge that it is working. Update your vision board to represent new dreams and goals. You can date your vision board and create new ones showing your progress.

Much like a time capsule, your saved vision boards will document your personal journey, your dreams, and your achievements for that particular year. It will become a record of your growth, awareness and expansion that you will want to keep and reflect back upon in years to come.

As you continue to grow, evolve and expand, your dreams will too. Your vision board will always be there keeping track of it all. It will chronicle your dreams, your growth and your achievements.

Here are some daily actions you should follow with your vision board:

Look at your vision board often and feel the inspiration it provides.
Hold it in your hands and really internalize the future it represents.
Read your affirmations and inspirational words aloud.
See yourself living in that manner.
Feel yourself in the future you have designed.
Believe it is already yours.
Be grateful for the good that is already present in your life.
Acknowledge any goals you have already achieved.
Acknowledge the changes you have seen and felt.
Acknowledge the Law of Attraction at work in your life.
Look at it just before going to bed and first thing upon rising.

Your ability to visualize your dreams will serve as a catalyst in their creation.

10. THE FOUR QUESTIONS

I do not know what you are focused on but if you are not getting the results you would like to have, chances are you need a new strategy. Which also means you need to focus on something else.

Here are four questions that will put you on the right track. You should be asking yourself these questions everyday and working on them everyday.

118

1. What did you do last week to make yourself smarter this week?

2. What are you doing this week to make yourself smarter next week?

Yes, this is about personal development and it's an ongoing process. Simply stated, what are you doing to make yourself a better person? You could be reading to increase your level of awareness, to learn to love more and hate less, learn to have more patience with yourself and the people around you. Anything that you can do to make yourself a better person is what you should be working on.

I said this earlier and it is worth repeating, I find it hard to believe that we are only here to work jobs we don't really like just to pay bills and then go out and party with friends every weekend. I believe and know there is more to life than that, and it is about knowing what you want and then developing ourselves so we can go and do bigger and better things.

Now the next two questions:

3. How much money would you like to have on your bank account when you are 65?

THINK BIG here. And remember, age doesn't matter. What matters is you think outside the box because anything is possible. So, would you like to have €300.000, €500.000 or maybe €1.000.000 euros or more in your bank account by the time you are 65? You've decided? Thats great! And now...

4. What are you doing right now to make that happen?

You might think this is an impossible task. Trust me, it's not. Remember what I said earlier, "Successful people are not people without problems. Successful people are people who learn to find solutions to their problems."

Almost everyone I know would like to have an extra €10,000 euro a month coming in but how many people are willing to do something to actually make that happen? Are you ready to do something? Are you willing to work for it? Because I am not going to give it to you for free, and no one else is going to going to give it to you for free either. Yes, you could try to win it but chances are you would lose more money trying. So it's really going to be about how important it is to you and are you willing to legally work for it.

You may have to change your job. Heck, you may have to first get a job. You may have to get creative, you may have to learn something new, you may have to move. You may have to learn to be more patience with yourself while working towards your goal. But you will have to take some kind of action.

The idea is to take action to make things happen in your life. There are people making €10.000 euro a month, there are people who beginning with 65 or 70 years of age start new careers and begin making €100.000 euro a year and more. If its possible for other people to do it then it means you can do it too. But it's not going to happen if you are sitting around on your butt doing nothing but watching TV and partying with your friends.

Now, re-read questions 1 and 2.

11. UNDERSTAND THE LAW OF COMPENSATION

Lets talk about money. It is a concept that is largely misunderstood by many people. Most of what we have learned about money is wrong, therefore we don't talk about it much. Many people believe money is that stuff that other people are suppose to have. Some people will tell you that they don't need money because, "Well, money won't make you happy." That's just silly. First, people who say they don't need money are people who haven't learned how to earn it. Second money isn't there to make you happy, it's there to make you comfortable.

Here is what I told my son about money:

"Money is not meant to make you happy, it's there to make you comfortable. So if money doesn't make you happy then it doesn't matter if you have it. If it doesn't matter whether you have it or not then you may as well have it. That way when you are not happy at least you are comfortable."

To give you a better idea; I have a very nice place where I live. If I come home and I am not in happy mood I can sit comfortably in my place, relax, and put myself in the right frame of mind to make great things happen. You get the idea right?

Here is what you need to know about money. It is, has been and always will be based on the service that you provide. And you may not receive it from same source. You may provide excellence service for Company A but receive your compensation from Company H. If you provide great service you will be compensated for it because that's the law. The Law of Compensation states that the satisfaction, money and rewards you receive in life will be based on:

1. The need for what you do.
2. Your ability to do it.
3. The difficulty there will be in replacing you.

Is there a need for what you do? Are you doing something that truly helps other people? Something people can benefit from and obtain satisfaction? In my work I understand there is a need for what I do. People are confused and looking for answers on how to change things in their lives. They have tried things over and over again with no success. My job is to provide new strategies to make great things happen in their lives. To show them ways to be do or have anything they want.

Next up is your ability to do what you do. How good can you do your job? How much time are you investing in yourself so you can do your job better? This goes back to the first two questions listed under the section The Four Questions. You should be asking yourself these questions on a regular basis.

Now if there is a need for what you do and you are constantly working on your ability to do it; to be the best you can be, then that will take care of point number three, the difficulty there will be in placing you.

If you are providing an excellent service or a great product, what will happen when you stop doing so? Will you be greatly missed? If so, then this is when the service or product you provide starts to really make a profit for you. It's about people having an interest in what you do. They like your style, your way of doing things. It means people are willing to buy your product or use your service because no one can do it the way YOU do it.

Here is an example of the law of compensation at work.

I am your classic Renaissance Man. Among the many things I do, I am also a DJ/Event Manager for the Vault Social Club. It's a private group that focuses on beautiful people, great music, all the time. The idea is to create safe and stress free environment to relax, dance and have fun with friends.

A few years back I used to DJ at this bar in the city. Now there are a lot of DJs out there but I have my own soulful American style music mix. I play great music with a funk and soul vibe that people really enjoy listening and dancing to. It's something that is missing and I am able to provide it. I love what I was do. A lot of people love what I do and the way I do it. **It's my ability to do it** that puts me in high demand.

Bar A paid me for my services. It equaled out to some pocket change and a few few drinks at the bar for me and my guests. I always did a great job, no matter what. Whether a small crowd, or large, private event or New Years Eve special, I gave a 110% performance. Now, my salary at Bar A did not increase, but many people who were enjoying my style wanted me to play at their events and that's when my salary increased. Company E and Club H would pay me 4 to 5 times more for one evening than Club A would for a whole weekend. Law of compensation states if you are doing a great service you will be compensated for it. It may not be at the same place but you will receive compensation because that's a law.

Some time later I left Bar A, simply because it was time for me to move on to bigger and better things. Every now and then I meet up with people who say „I remember you from Bar A! We really missed that weekend dance groove you did there. Are you still playing that cool funky music and what's this I keep hearing about The Vault Social Club?" – **that's the need for what I do**.

When I left Bar A, some people stopped going there because the style was different and they didn't enjoy it as much - **the difficulty there was in replacing me**.

Once you learn how the Law of Compensation works, it gets even better. If you want to make more money expand your service. You want less money reduce your service.

12. IT IS WHAT IT IS

Sometimes things just happen.

Whatever happens in life, it is what it is, accept it.
1. You control it or it controls you.
2. Harvest the good. There is good in everything.
3. Let it go. Forgive and let it go.

13. ALWAYS BELIEVE IN YOURSELF

No matter what it is you want in life, better fitness and health, loving relationships, more money, the first person who has to believe you can achieve these things is YOU. You won't need a "Plan B", because it will distract you from Plan A - believing in yourself.

There will be some tough times ahead of you. It will test your character, patience and make you wonder if it is really worth it.

124

Trust me it's worth it, it's your life. You deserve to have great things happen to you. But it won't happen just by sitting around dreaming, you will have to take ACTION on your dreams to make them happen.

So when the going gets tough and it will, what is the one thing that can always keep you focused? That one thing that will make sure you stay in the game of life and keep you moving forward toward your goals? What is that key? Always tell yourself...

14. IT'S POSSIBLE

At the moment you may not know how, but you do know it's possible. If other people can make their dreams come true then YOU can make your dreams come true. You will have to practice new techniques. You may have to find a mentor, or be a part of a support group; maybe even create your own support team of people who are doing the things you want to do. It's important to have people that can help you on your way and not people who stand in your way.

Give your ideas and dreams a chance. Believe that you are ready for the next step. In life, it's rarely about getting a chance, it's about taking a chance. You'll never be 100% sure it will work, but you can always be 100% sure doing nothing won't work. You are ready! Think about it. You have everything you need right now to take the next small, realistic step forward. So embrace the opportunities that come your way, and accept the challenges – they're gifts that will help you to grow. Either you succeed or you learn something. A Win-Win situation.

15. WAKE UP 30 MINUTES EARLY EVERY MORNING

Get up 30 minutes earlier than usual so you don't have to rush around like a mad crazy person. That 30 minutes will help you avoid speeding tickets, avoid being late and other unnecessary headaches. Do it for 30 days straight and see how it impacts your life.

16. EVERY MORNING WATCH OR READ SOMETHING THAT INSPIRES YOU

Sometimes all you need is a little pep talk. For the next 30 days, before you eat breakfast, or leave the house, watch a motivational video or read something (quotation, blog post, short story, etc.) that inspires you. One suggestion would be to check out: www.wellandgoodlifestyle.de for inspiration and motivation.

17. EXERCISE FOR 15 MINUTES EVERYDAY FOR 30 DAYS

Your health is your life. Don't let it go. Eat right, exercise and get an annual physical check-up. By using 1% of your day for fitness, which is only 15 minutes, you can transform your body. I am a fitness enthusiast and a big fan of bodyweight training. You can train anywhere, anytime, no excuses. If you are interested in taking your fitness to the next level then follow the www.wellandgoodlifestyle.de link. They provide connections to cool workout sessions and retreats.

18. BE HONEST WITH YOURSELF
ABOUT EVERYTHING

Be honest about what's right, as well as what needs to be changed. Be honest about what you want to achieve and who you want to become. Be honest with every aspect of your life, always. Search your soul, for the truth, so that you truly know who you are. Once you do, you'll have a better understanding of where you are now and how you got here, and you'll be better equipped to identify where you want to go and how to get there. Be yourself, genuinely and proudly. Trying to be anyone else is a waste of the person you are. Embrace that individual inside you that has ideas, strengths and beauty like no one else. Be the person you know yourself to be – the best version of you – on your terms. Above all, be true to YOU. You have a goal to achieve something great. But if you cannot put your heart in it, stop and be honest with yourself about it. It's all feedback. Make the necessary adjustments and go make great things happen.

19. BE MORE POLITE TO YOURSELF

Another reminder to take better care of yourself. If you had a friend who spoke to you in the same bad way that you sometimes speak to yourself, how long would you allow that person to be your friend? The way you should treat yourself is with the same respect you treat others. You must love who you are or no one else will.

20. DEFINE ONE LONG TERM GOAL AND WORK ON IT FOR AN HOUR EVERY DAY

Break your goal down into bite-sized pieces and focus on achieving each piece, one at a time. It really is all about taking baby steps, and taking the first step is often the hardest. Always remember, the journey of a thousand miles begins with one step. Get out there and DO something! The harder you work the luckier you will become. While many of us decide at some point during the course of our lives that we want to answer our calling, to do that thing we truly enjoy doing, only a small group of us actually work on it. By 'working on it,' I mean consistently devoting oneself to the end result. Spend an hour every day for the next 30 days working toward something you've always wanted to accomplish. Take a small dream and make it a reality.

21. CONCENTRATE ON BEING POSITIVE AT ALL TIMES

The real winners in life cultivate optimism. No matter what the situation, the successful person is the person who will always find a way to put an optimistic spin on it. The mind must believe it can do something before it is capable of actually doing it. The way to overcome negative thoughts and destructive emotions is to develop positive emotions that are stronger and more powerful. Listen to your self-talk and replace negative thoughts with positive ones. Regardless of how a situation seems, focus on what you want, and then take the next positive step forward. No, you can't control everything that happens to you, but you can control how you react to things. Each and everyone of us has positive and negative aspects – and whether or not you're happy and successful in the long run depends greatly on which aspects you focus on.

22. LET GO OF ONE RELATIONSHIP THAT CONSTANTLY HURTS YOU

Let go of one relationship that constantly hurts you. This is very important. You want to have people who can help you on your way and not stand in your way. Keep people in your life who truly love you, motivate you, encourage you, enhance you, and make you happy.

If you know people who do none of these things, let them go and make room for new positive relationships. Over the next 30 days, if relevant to your situation, gradually let go of one person in your life who has been continuously hurting you and holding you back.

23. FORGIVE YOURSELF AND OTHERS

We've all been hurt by our own decisions and by the decisions of others. And while the pain of these experiences is normal, sometimes it lingers for too long. We relive the pain over and over and have a hard time letting go. Forgiveness is the key remedy. It doesn't mean you're erasing the past, or forgetting what happened. It means you're letting go of the resentment and pain, and instead choosing to learn from the incident and move on with your life.

24. START VALUING THE LESSONS
YOUR MISTAKES TEACH YOU

Mistakes are okay. They're the stepping stones of progress. If you're not failing from time to time, you're not trying hard enough and you're not learning. Take risks, stumble, fall, and then get up and try again. Appreciate that you are pushing yourself, learning, growing and improving. Significant achievements are almost invariably realized at the end of a long road of failures. One of the 'mistakes' you fear might just be the link to your greatest achievement yet.

25. EVENINGS REFLECT ON
HOW YOUR DAY WENT

Spend 10 minutes every evening reflecting on what went well. For the next 30 days spend 10 minutes every evening pondering the small successes that occurred during the course of the day. This process of positive reflection will remind you of all the tiny blessings in your life, and help you to celebrate your personal growth.

As you progress through these challenges remember, personal growth is a slow, steady process. It can't be rushed. You need to work on it gradually every day. There is enough time for you to be who you want to be in life. Don't settle for less than what you think you deserve, or less than you know you can be. Despite the struggles you'll face along the way, never give up on yourself. You're braver than you believe, stronger than you seem, smarter than you think, and twice as capable as you have ever imagined.

Things Successful People Don't Do

With work, play, relationships, money; what makes people successful? Well, they know that success is the progressive realization of a worthy idea. They know that at different times in their lives they have achieved success more than once and constantly continue to build upon that. They also know that they have to find solutions to their problems.

Successful people have a very positive attitude and not some magical power that you don't have. So, instead of letting stress control them, these people take control of their life by managing stress and striving to improve every day. They manage their emotions, thoughts, and behaviors in ways that set them up for success in life.

So, to be successful, there are certain things successful people just don't do...

1. They Don't Assume the Worst.
It's amazing how many problems wouldn't exist if we didn't invent them. Successful people know that leaping to conclusions is usually a bad idea. Instead of freaking out about an unanswered text ("What if they don't like me?"), they go on with their day ("hmm, they must be busy!"). Before they decide that another person is untrustworthy, they make an honest effort to find out more about them.

2. They Don't Resist the Truth.
It's easy to live in a lie because lies can grow so strong that it can eventually make people forget about the truth. Successful people know that they need to face the truth and live with it be-

cause making excuses will never get a solution for what has gone wrong.

3. They Don't Hold On To Resentment.
Successful people understand that resentment only causes pain in life over and over again, so they let go of it. They choose to accept and forgive things happened in the past and move on with their lifes. They use what they have learned from these past incidents.

4. They Don't Forget the Little Things.
Is it easy to forget the little things? Certainly. But successful people don't make a habit of it. Instead, they express gratitude for every blessing, no matter how big or small. They know it's silly to think more stuff will make them feel better if they can't be happy about what they have.

5. They Don't Pass the Blame on to Something Else
Successful people realize they are the CEO of their life and thus take full responsibility for how things are. They didn't get "stuck in traffic" — they were late. They didn't "have something come up" — they forgot. Successful people don't claim "they can't help it," because they can do anything they set their mind to.

6. They Don't See Problems as "Problems".
The word "problems" is seen as "challenges" for successful people. They believe that every obstacle comes as an opportunity that is yet to be discovered. Successful people take the chance to challenge themselves and improve their life.

7. They Don't Resign Themselves to "Reality."
This "reality" most people speak of sounds like a dreadful place

where dreams go to die. Successful people know that anything is possible with consistency and hustle, so they choose to write their own reality.

8. They Don't Expect Something for Nothing.

Successful people don't fall for "lose weight fast" or "get rich quick" scams. They know that anything worth having requires hard work (often, lots of it). Successful people are comfortable with the fact that achieving success might take a bit longer than they would like but know will be so worth it.

9. They Don't Get Bored.

Boredom is a place where creativity, inspiration, and productivity die. Successful people are fascinated by everything around them. They explore the world with enthusiasm and curiosity, asking as many questions as they can.

10. They Don't Let Negative Thoughts Hijack Their Brain.

Successful people don't subject themselves to a chorus of self-defeating negative thoughts. When a negative thought passes through their head, they remind themselves: if I wouldn't say it about another person, I shouldn't think it about myself.

11. They Don't Make Comparison With Others.

Successful people understand that everyone is different and has his own progress, so they don't compare themselves with other people. They are confident about what they have and what they do. Instead of focusing on how others are doing, they pay attention on how to improve their own life.

12. They Don't Agonize Over Every Little Mistake.
Successful people don't look at failure as a terrible thing to avoid at all costs. They know that failure is a possibility when it comes to trying anything new. Seeing failure for what it is, a learning opportunity and nothing more, helps positive people achieve massive success as they learn and grow.

13. They Don't Think Life Is Perfect.
Successful people forget about perfection, because it's just not possible. When is the last time you thought, "Wow, this is the perfect day to get in shape," or "You know what? This is the day I quit my job, move to Santa Fe, and pursue my real passion?" Oh, that's right: you didn't, because there isn't a "perfect time" to do anything. Successful people take action in the here and now, perfection be damned.

14. They Don't Hang Out with Toxic People.
Successful people don't let negative, toxic people drag them down. Instead, they surround themselves with other successful people who are fun and inspiring to be with. **Why should a successful person spend their time with a person who complains about everything, gossips about everybody and only has ideas on how things will not work?** Trust me, they don't.

15. They Don't Waste Time Feeling Sorry for Themselves.
Successful people are mentally strong people and they don't sit around feeling sorry about their circumstances or how others have treated them. Instead, they take responsibility for their role in life and understand that life isn't always easy or fair.

16. They Don't Give Away Their Power.
They don't allow others to control them, and they don't give someone else power over them. They don't say things like, "My boss makes me feel bad," because they understand that they are in control over their own emotions and they have a choice in how they respond.

17. They Don't Shy Away from Change.
Successful people don't try to avoid change. Instead, they welcome positive change and are willing to be flexible. They understand that change is inevitable and believe in their abilities to adapt.

18. They Don't Waste Energy on Things They Can't Control.
You won't hear a successful, mentally strong person complaining over lost luggage or traffic jams. Instead, they focus on what they can control in their lives. They recognize that sometimes, the only thing they can control is their attitude.

19. They Don't Worry About Pleasing Everyone.
Successful people recognize that they don't need to please everyone all the time. They're not afraid to say no or speak up when necessary. They strive to be kind and fair, but can handle other people being upset if they didn't make them happy.

20. They Don't Fear Taking Calculated Risks.
They don't take reckless or foolish risks, but don't mind taking calculated risks. Successful people spend time weighing the risks and benefits before making a big decision, and they're fully informed of the potential downsides before they take action.

21. They Don't Dwell on the Past.

Successful people don't waste time dwelling on the past and wishing things could be different. They acknowledge their past and can say what they've learned from it. However, they don't constantly relive bad experiences or fantasize about the glory days. Instead, they live for the present and plan for the future.

22. They Don't Make the Same Mistakes Over and Over.

Successful people accept responsibility for their behavior and learn from their past mistakes. As a result, they don't keep repeating those mistakes over and over. Instead, they move on and make better decisions in the future.

23. They Don't Resent Other People's Success.

Successful people can appreciate and celebrate other people's success in life. They don't grow jealous or feel cheated when others surpass them. Instead, they recognize that success comes with hard work and they are willing to work hard for their own chance at success.

24. They Don't Give Up After the First Failure.

Successful people don't view failure as a reason to give up. Instead, they use failure as an opportunity to grow and improve. They are willing to keep trying until they get it right.

25. They Don't Fear Alone Time.

Successful people can tolerate being alone and they don't fear silence. They aren't afraid to be alone with their thoughts and they can use downtime to be productive. They enjoy their own company and aren't dependent on others for companionship and entertainment all the time but instead can be happy alone.

26. They Don't Feel the World Owes Them Anything.
Successful people don't feel entitled to things in life. They weren't born with a mentality that others would take care of them or that the world must give them something. Instead, they look for opportunities based on their own merits.

27. They Don't Expect Immediate Results.
Whether they are working on improving their health or getting a new business off the ground, successful people don't expect immediate results. Instead, they apply their skills and time to the best of their ability and understand that real change takes time.

Knowledge is important. The key is "taking action." Now you know. Take action.

Courage or Conformity

The late Earl Nightingale was, for many years, the most listened to man on radio. His radio show, "Our Changing World" was broadcast on over 1,000 radio stations around the world. He researched and wrote every show himself. The man virtually devoured books. He was consumed with the idea of why so few people succeed in life and so many others do. I've had the good fortune of studying a lot of Earl Nightingale's work. It is simple, straight forward and honest. A tremendous, eye opening learning experience.

We all admire the courageous person and quite often consider the individual who lacks courage, a loser or a coward. However, that is not how Earl Nightingale saw it. He said the opposite of courage was not cowardliness, it was conformity.

What is conformity? Conformity involves changing your behaviors in order to "fit in" or "go along" with the people around you. Suppose, for example, you go with friends to see a film. You didn't think the film was very good, but all your friends thought that it was absolutely brilliant. You might be tempted to conform by pretending to agree with their verdict on the film rather than being the odd one out." Ask a person "Why they go to work?" The answer is usually "Well everyone has to go to work so they can pay the bills." That's not a very good answer. But everyone is doing what everyone else is doing because that's what everyone does.

I believe the more you think about that, the more you will be inclined to agree that conformity is a big problem. It takes courage to break away from the crowd, to go your own way, to do the thing that may be unpopular. It takes courage to stand

138

up for the person who is being unjustly criticized, rather than agreeing and going along with the crowd. It takes courage for the teenager to say no, when all the rest of the kids begin going down the wrong path.

Earl Nightingale was correct, the opposite of courage is conformity. It is one reason so few people enjoy any lasting success. It is so easy to go along with the large group. We don't have to stand out. We don't have to be different. We just go with the flow.

What are you going to do? To do your thing, to achieve your greatness will mean as you grow you will break away from the crowd and go your way. Yes, you will leave people behind but you will meet new people who understand you and can support you on your journey to greatness. Are you ready? Because, right now is the time for to start taking action. Be courageous and go your own way. There is no compensation in conformity.

How Not To Be Offended

On your journey to greatness, this will be of great importance to you.

There is an ancient and well-kept secret to happiness which the Great Ones have known for centuries. They rarely talk about it, but they use it all the time, and it is fundamental to good mental health. This secret is called The Fine Art of Not Being Offended.

In order to truly be a master of this art, one must be able to see that every statement, action and reaction of another human being is the sum result of their total life experience to date. In other words, the majority of people in our world say and do what they do from their own set of fears, conclusions, defenses and attempts to survive. Most of it, even when aimed directly at us, has nothing to do with us. Usually, it has to do with all those other times a person has had an experience, perhaps when they were young and now they are taking it out on you. Sometimes it happens that "hurt people", hurt people.

So, truth be told almost nothing is personal.

Even with our closest loved ones, our beloved partners, our children and our friends. We are all swimming in the projections and filters of each other's life experiences and often we are just the stand-ins, the chess pieces of life to which our loved ones have their own built-in reactions. I am not trying to dehumanize life or take away the intimacy from our relationships, but it is important for us to know that almost every time we get offended, we are actually just in a misunderstanding.

Knowing this actually allows for more intimacy and less

suffering throughout all of our relationships. Because now you know that at any given time you could be standing in the right place at the right time for someone to say or do something that's incorrect or inappropriate and you don't have to take it personally. If it wasn't you, it would likely be someone else.

This will actually allow you to be a little more detached from the reactions of people around you. How often does it happen that you react to a statement of another by being offended rather than seeing that the other might actually be hurting? That the other person has a problem, has no solution and possibly no desire in finding a solution.

In fact, every time you get offended, it is actually an opportunity to extend kindness to the one who may be suffering, even if they themselves do not appear that way on the surface. All anger, all acting out, all harshness, all criticism, is in truth a form of suffering. When you provide no Velcro for it to stick, something changes in the world. We do not even have to say a thing. **In fact, it is usually better not to say a thing**. People who are suffering on the inside, but not showing it on the outside, are usually not pleased when someone points out to them that they are suffering. You do not need to be everyone's therapist. But you do need to understand the situation and move on. In this way you experience less suffering and at best, you have a chance to make the world a better place.

And when you know that nothing is personal, a magical thing happens. Many of the people who offend and abuse you will start to leave your life. Once you are conscious of this, you can only be offended if you believe what the other people are saying. When you know nothing is personal, you do not end up feeling abused or offended. All you have to say is, "Thank you for sharing that," and move on. You are no longer hooked in by what another person does or says, because you know it is not about you.

Your self worth is not determined by what another person says, does or believes. You can make your life easier now because you do not have to convince other people that you are a good and worthy person.

The great challenge of life is to live your life as you wish regardless of what other people do, say, think or believe. The fine art of not being offended is one of the many skills practiced by success people in every area of their lives. Though it may take a lifetime of practice, it is truly one of the best kept secrets for living a happy life.

Conclusion
(but this is actually the beginning)

A great journey awaits you because now you have your personal power. You now know you can be, do or have ANYTHING you want. You just have to take action to improve your life.

First and foremost, I want to thank you for your time. My mission here was to share this simple yet powerful information with you. There is an art and science to success. If you change your way of thinking, yes it will change your life.

Do these techniques work? Of course they do. How do I know? Because I have taken this information, studied it and practiced it everyday. I have shared it with others and they too have benefited from practicing these techniques. Personally, I have achieved some really outstanding results in my life. One of which you are holding in your hands, this book.

Writing this was a long hard journey and I am thankful for the experience. For years I have been fascinated with the idea of being an author. I have always wanted to write and publish my own books, and now that I have started I can tell you that other books are on the way.

There was a time when I didn't know how but I knew it was possible, so I never lost the passion. And once I started to change my way of thinking, a whole new way of seeing the world was opened up to me. Understanding and learning how to use my personal power is the key to my success. I begin to believe in myself and then I took action. Now it's your turn. And I know you can do this.

Always remember...

You were born with
PERSONAL POWER
To be, do or have ANYTHING you want
and
Whether you think you can,
or whether you think can't,
you're right.

I wish you well on your journey to increasing your personal power.

And don't forget to enjoy the scenery along the way.

From my mind to your mind.
Love, Peace & Soul,

Homier